THE ABC OF COMMUNITY LAW

(Fourth edition)

By Dr Klaus-Dieter Borchardt
Manuscript completed in October 1993
Cover: Graphic design by Finn Nygaard

Cataloguing data can be found at the end of this publication

Luxembourg: Office for Official Publications of the European Communities, 1994

ISBN 92-826-6293-4

© ECSC-EC-EAEC, Brussels • Luxembourg, 1994
Reproduction is authorized, except for commercial purposes, provided the source is acknowledged.

Printed in Germany Printed on white chlorine-free paper

CONTENTS

INTRODUCTION	5
THE 'CONSTITUTION' OF THE EUROPEAN COMMUNITY	7
■ STRUCTURE OF THE COMMUNITY	7
Tasks — Powers — Legal character	
■ FUNDAMENTAL VALUES OF THE COMMUNITY	12
Peace — Unity — Equality — Freedom — Solidarity — Economic and social security — Fundamental rights	
■ THE INSTITUTIONS OF THE COMMUNITY	17
European Council — European Parliament — Council — Commission Court of Justice — Court of Auditors — Ancillary bodies	
THE COMMUNITY AS A LEGAL REALITY	32
■ THE COMMUNITY IS CREATED BY LAW	32
■ THE COMMUNITY IS A LEGAL ORDER	33
■ THE LEGAL SOURCES OF COMMUNITY LAW	34
The founding treaties — Community legal instruments — The Community's range of tools — Community laws — Directives and ECSC recommendations — Administrative decisions — Recommendations and opinions — International agreements — The EEA — General principles of law — Agreements between the Member States	
■ THE LEGISLATIVE PROCESS IN THE COMMUNITY	44
The proposal procedure — The cooperation procedure — The co-decision procedure — The procedure for implementing measures — The simplified procedure — Specific ECSC procedures	
■ LEGALITY OF THE ACTS OF THE INSTITUTIONS	51
■ COMMUNITY SYSTEM OF LEGAL PROTECTION	51
Treaty infringement proceedings — Actions for annulment — Complaints for failure to act — Actions for damages — Actions by Community staff — Preliminary ruling procedure	

THE POSITION OF COMMUNITY LAW IN RELATION TO THE LEGAL ORDER AS A WHOLE — 55

- THE AUTONOMY OF THE COMMUNITY LEGAL ORDER — 55
- COOPERATION BETWEEN COMMUNITY LAW AND NATIONAL LAW — 57
- CONFLICT BETWEEN COMMUNITY LAW AND NATIONAL LAW — 58
  Direct applicability of Community law — Primacy of Community law

CONCLUSIONS — 63

TABLE OF CASES — 64

FURTHER READING — 67

INTRODUCTION

Until shortly after the end of the Second World War our concept of the State and our political life had developed almost entirely on the basis of national constitutions and laws. It was on this basis in our democratic States that the rules of conduct binding not only on citizens and parties but also on the State and its organs were created. It took the complete collapse of Europe to give a new impetus to the idea of a new European order, at least in Western Europe. The foundation stone of a European Community was laid by the then French Foreign Minister Robert Schuman in his declaration of 9 May 1950, in which he put forward the plan he had worked out with Jean Monnet to pool Europe's coal and steel industries. By this means, he declared, a historic initiative would be taken for an organized and vital Europe, which was indispensable for civilization and without which the peace of the world could not be maintained. This plan became a reality with the conclusion of the founding Treaty of the European Coal and Steel Community (ECSC) on 18 April 1951 in Paris and its entry into force on 23 July 1952. A further development came some years later with the Treaties of Rome of 25 March 1957, which created the European Economic Community (EEC) and the European Atomic Energy Community (Euratom). The founding States of these Communities were Belgium, the Federal Republic of Germany, France, Italy, Luxembourg and the Netherlands. On 1 January 1973 Denmark, Ireland and the United Kingdom of Great Britain and Northern Ireland acceded to the Community; the accession of Norway, which had been planned to take place at the same time, was rejected by a referendum in October 1972. In 1976 and 1977 Greece, Portugal and Spain submitted applications to join the Community. This 'southward extension' of the Community was completed with the accession of Spain and Portugal on 1 January 1986, Greece having already become a member on 1 January 1981. Twelve European States are now united in the Community. Applications for membership have been made by Turkey (1987), Austria (1989), Cyprus (1990), Malta (1990), Sweden (1991), Finland (1991), Switzerland (1992) and Norway (1992).

Since the entry into force of the Treaties of Rome on 1 January 1958 three separate Communities have existed, each based on its own founding instruments. From a legal point of view this situation has remained unchanged to the present day, since no formal merger of the three Communities has ever taken place. There are however good reasons for regarding these three Communities, different as they are in the fields they cover, as constituting one unit so far as their political and legal structure is concerned. They have been set up by the same Member States and are based on the same fundamental objectives, as expressed in the preambles to the three Treaties: to create 'an organized and vital Europe', 'to lay the foundations of an ever closer union among the peoples of Europe', and to combine their efforts to 'contribute ... to the prosperity of their peoples'. This approach was also adopted in the resolution of the European Parliament of 16 February 1978, which proposed that the three Communities should be designated 'the European Community'. Common usage too, both in the media and in everyday life, has long since come to regard the three Communities as one. The Treaty on European Union (Maastricht Treaty), signed by the Heads of State or Government of the Member States in February 1992, provides for the expression 'European Community' to replace 'European Economic Community'. The EEC Treaty becomes the EC Treaty.[1] The point is

---

[1] For ease of reference, where Articles of the former EEC Treaty have been renumbered in the new EC Treaty, the old numbers are indicated in a footnote beginning with an asterisk (*).

to reinforce perceptions of the qualitative transition from a Community with primarily economic purposes to a fuller political union. For simplicity's sake this booklet refers throughout to the European Community (EC), but in a slightly different sense, looking at all three Communities (ECSC, EEC, Euratom) as an aggregate, which goes further than even the Maastricht Treaty.

The legal order created by the European Community has already become an established component of our political life. Each year, on the basis of the Community treaties, thousands of decisions are taken that crucially affect the lives of the Community's Member States and of their citizens. The individual has long since ceased to be merely a citizen of his town, district or State; he is also a Community citizen. For this reason alone it is of the highest importance that the Community citizen should be informed about the legal order that affects him personally. Yet the complexities of the Community and its legal order are not easy for the citizen to grasp. This is partly due to the wording of the treaties themselves, which is often somewhat obscure and the implications of which are not easy to discern. An additional factor is the unfamiliarity of many concepts with which the treaties sought to break new ground. The following pages are an attempt to clarify the structure of the Community and the supporting pillars of the European legal order, and thus help to lessen the incomprehension prevailing among Community citizens.

THE 'CONSTITUTION' OF THE EUROPEAN COMMUNITY

Every social organization has a constitution. By means of a constitution the structure of a political system is defined, that is to say the relationship of the various parts to each other and to the whole is specified, the common objectives are defined and the rules for making binding decisions are laid down. The constitution of the European Community, as an association of States to which quite specific tasks and functions have been allotted, must thus be able to answer the same questions as the constitution of a State.

This Community constitution is not, as in the case of most of the constitutions of its Member States, laid down in a comprehensive constitutional document, but arises from the totality of rules and fundamental values by which those in authority regard themselves as bound. These rules are to be found partly in the founding treaties or in the legal instruments produced by the Community institutions, but they also rest partly on custom.

In the Member States the body politic is shaped by two overriding principles: the rule of law and democracy. All the activities of the Community, if they are to be true to the fundamental requirements of law and democracy, must be both legally and democratically legitimated: foundation, construction, competence, operation, the position of the Member States and their institutions and the position of the citizen.

What answers, then, does the Community order afford to these questions concerning its structure, its fundamental values and its institutions?

> The text of this publication was completed on 15th November 1993. It, therefore, does not include details of institutional changes after that date.

■ STRUCTURE OF THE COMMUNITY

The tasks of the Community

In its structure the Community order resembles the constitutional order of a State. This is immediately apparent from the list of tasks entrusted to the Community. These are not the narrowly circumscribed technical tasks commonly assumed by international organizations, but fields of competence which, taken as a whole, form essential attributes of statehood. Under the ECSC Treaty the Community is competent for the Community-wide administration of the coal and steel industries, which play a key role in the national economies. The European Atomic Energy Community has common tasks to perform in research for, and utilization of, atomic energy. Finally, the EEC does not aim, like the other two Communities, at the closer interlocking of specific sectors of the economy (so-called economic integration).

Rather, its task is, by establishing a common market that unites the national markets of the Member States and on which all goods and services can be offered and sold on the same conditions as on an internal market, and by the gradual approximation of the national economic policies in all sectors of the economy, to weld the Member States into a community. Specific matters covered are free movement of goods, free movement of workers, freedom of establishment, freedom to provide services and freedom of capital movements and payments, agriculture, transport policy, social policy and competition. Only a few, albeit important, aspects of State sovereignty are withheld from the Community, such as defence, diplomacy, education and culture; but even in these spheres certain partial aspects are subject to Community competence.

The concept of establishing a common market has been revitalized by the programme aimed at completion of the internal market by 1992. This programme was born of the realization that, on the one hand, there remained a series of national obstacles to the full establishment of the freedoms on which the common market is based and that, on the other hand, important sectors of the economy such as telecommunications and public procurement were not included in the common market. In its White Paper on the completion of the internal market, the Commission of the European Communities presented the Heads of State or Government of the (then) 10 Member States in June 1985 with some 300 proposals for legal instruments, complete with a detailed timetable, designed to remove all intra-Community barriers by the end of 1992. At the Milan Summit in the same year, the Heads of State or Government entrusted the Commission with the political task of implementing the single market programme. However, to achieve in just seven years what fewer Member States had failed to achieve in nearly three decades, a mere declaration of political intent and the adoption of a programme was not enough: the substance of Project 1992 had to be incorporated into the Treaties of Rome. This was done by the Single European Act, which added to the EEC Treaty, among other new provisions, an Article 8a* stipulating that the Community should take all the necessary measures to establish the internal market progressively by 31 December 1992. This provision entered into force along with the rest of the Single European Act on 1 July 1987.

The Treaty on European Union, which finally came into force in 1993 after the last remaining obstacles to ratification in a few Member States had been removed, carries the EC forward to a new economic and political dimension. This European Union will be built under a single institutional roof standing on three pillars:

Pillar 1: the three European Communities (EC, Euratom, ECSC), which are to be deepened and to have an economic and monetary union added to them;

Pillar 2: cooperation between the Member States in the common foreign and security policy;

Pillar 3: cooperation between the Member States in justice and home affairs.

It will have the following new tasks and objectives:

(i) to promote economic and social progress which is balanced and sustainable, in particular through the creation of an area without internal frontiers, through the strengthening of economic and social cohesion and through the establishment of an economic and monetary union, ultimately including a single currency;

(ii) to assert its identity on the international scene, in particular through the implementation of a common foreign and security policy, including the eventual framing of a common defence policy;

(iii) to strengthen the protection of the rights and interests of the nationals of its Member States through the introduction of Union citizenship;

(iv) to develop close cooperation on justice and home affairs and

(v) to maintain in full the *acquis communautaire* and to build on it.

The powers of the Community

The similarities between the Community order and that of a State become even more striking if we consider the extent of the powers with which the Community institutions are endowed for the performance of the tasks entrusted to the Community. The founding treaties do not confer on the Community and its institutions any general power to take all measures necessary to achieve the objectives of the treaty, but lay down in each chapter the extent of the powers to act (principle of specific conferment of powers). This

---

* Now Article 7a of the EC Treaty.

method has been chosen by the Member States in order to ensure that the renunciation of their own powers can be more easily monitored and controlled. The range of matters covered by the specific conferments of power varies according to the nature of the tasks allotted to the Community. It is very far-reaching, for instance, in the common transport policy, where any appropriate provisions may be enacted (Article 75(1)(a) EC)*, in agricultural policy (Articles 43(2) and 40(3) EC) and in the sphere of freedom of movement of workers (Article 48 EC). On the other hand, in competition law (Article 85 *et seq.* EC) the scope for discretion on the part of the Community and its institutions is limited by narrowly defined conditions. In addition to these special powers to act, the Community treaties also confer on the institutions a power to act when this proves necessary to attain one of the objectives of the treaty (see Articles 235 EC, 203 Euratom, 95, first paragraph, ECSC — subsidiary power to act). These articles do not, however, confer on the institutions any general power enabling them to carry out tasks which lie outside the objectives laid down in the treaties. And the subsidiarity principle further debars the Community institutions from extending their powers to the detriment of those of the Member States. In practice, after initial hesitations, the possibilities afforded by this power have been used with increasing frequency. This is because the Community is nowadays confronted with tasks that were not foreseen at the time the founding treaties were concluded, and for which accordingly no appropriate powers were conferred in the treaties. Examples are the protection of the environment and of consumers, the establishment of a European Regional Fund as a means of closing the gap between the developed and underdeveloped regions of the Community, the establishment of the European Monetary Cooperation Fund and the numerous research programmes concluded since 1973 outside the European Atomic Energy Community. The Community was specifically given jurisdiction in these fields by the Single European Act. Finally, there are further powers to take such measures as are indispensable for the effective and meaningful implementation of powers that have already been expressly conferred (implied powers). These powers have acquired a special significance in the conduct of external relations. They enable the Community to assume obligations towards non-member States or other international organizations in fields covered by the list of tasks entrusted to the Community. An outstanding example is provided by the *Kramer* case decided by the Court of Justice of the European Communities. This case concerned the Community's capacity to cooperate with international organizations in fixing fishing quotas and, where thought appropriate, to assume obligations on the matter under international law. The Court inferred the necessary external competence of the Community from its competence for fisheries under the common agricultural policy.

The Treaty on European Union builds on the powers conferred on the three original Communities, extending and adding to them in a variety of respects. The European Economic Community (renamed the European Community by the Treaty on European Union) can now exercise new powers in relation to the internal market, economic policy and monetary policy, embracing all that this entails in social, cultural, research, political, environmental and development cooperation. Euratom's powers remain confined to the economic aspects of research and safety in relation to the peaceful use of nuclear energy and the common market in nuclear materials and equipment. The ECSC remains competent for questions affecting the common market in coal and steel. The Maastricht Treaty then adds specific powers for the European Union in matters of foreign and security policy and justice and home affairs.

---

* Formerly Article 75(i)(c) EEC.

But the exercise of these powers by the European Union is governed by the subsidiarity principle, taken over from Roman Catholic social doctrine, which has acquired virtually constitutional status. There are two facets to it: the affirmative statement that the EC must act where the objectives to be pursued can be better attained at Community level, which enhances its powers and the negative statement that it must not act where objectives can be satisfactorily attained by the Member States acting individually, which constrains them. What this means in practice is that all Community institutions, but especially the Commission, must always demonstrate that there is a real need for Community rules and common action. To paraphrase Montesquieu, when it is not necessary for the Community to take action, it is necessary that it should take none. If the need for Community rules is demonstrated, the next question that arises concerns the intensity and the form that they should take. The answer flows from the principle of proportionality that has entered Community law through the decisions of the Court of Justice. It means that the need for the specific legal instrument must be thoroughly assessed to see whether there is a less constraining means of achieving the same result. The chief conclusion to be reached in general terms is that framework legislation, minimum standards and mutual recognition of the Member States' existing standards should always be preferred to excessively detailed Community rules.

Legal character: The Community is not a State

These points of resemblance between the Community order and the national order of a State do not, however, suffice to confer on the Community the legal character of a (federal) State. Sovereign powers have been conferred on the Community institutions only in the limited spheres mentioned above, and those institutions have not been given any power to increase their competence merely by their own decisions. Thus, the Community lacks both the universal jurisdiction characteristic of a State and the power to create new fields of competence.

Even if the Community is not yet a State, it is certainly more developed than an organization set up under traditional international law. Its only essential point of similarity with traditional international organizations is the fact that it, too, was created by treaties taking effect under international law. But these treaties are at the same time the foundation documents establishing independent Communities endowed with their own sovereign rights and competence. The Member States have pooled certain parts of their own legislative powers in favour of these Communities and have placed them in the hands of Community institutions in which, however, they are given in return substantial rights of participation. The Community is thus a new form of relationship between States, something between a State in the traditional sense and an international organization. The concept of 'supranationality' has become accepted among lawyers as a means of describing their legal nature. This is intended to indicate that the Community is an association endowed with independent authority, with its own sovereign rights and a legal order independent of the Member States to which both the Member States and their citizens are subject in matters for which the Community is competent. It would, however, be wrong to infer that the European Community has thus already achieved its final form; on the contrary it is still a developing system, the ultimate contours of which are not yet predictable. This remains valid even after the entry into force of the Treaty on European Union. The Maastricht Treaty is not the end of the European Union's development process but simply a step further down the road

towards the ultimate goal. The fundamental economic and monetary policy areas are now anchored in the Union itself, and cooperation both on foreign and security policy and justice and home affairs are also institutionalized; but the EC as reorganized at Maastricht is as yet neither a unitary nor a federal State in the accepted sense of the words in international or constitutional law. Further progress in integration would be needed before that could come about, and for the moment there is little evidence that all those involved in the project are ready for it. There are still considerable differences of opinion on what the European Union is to be and do.

■ FUNDAMENTAL VALUES OF THE COMMUNITY

The foundations for constructing a united Europe were laid on fundamental ideas and values to which the Member States also subscribe and which are translated into practical reality by the Community's operational institutions. These acknowledged fundamental values include the securing of a lasting peace, unity, equality, freedom, solidarity, and economic and social security.

The Community as guarantor of peace

There is no motive for European unification that is surpassed by the desire for peace. In Europe, this century, two world wars have been waged between countries that are now Member States of the European Community. Thus, a policy for Europe means at the same time a policy for peace, and the establishment of the Community simultaneously created the centre-piece for a framework for peace in Europe that renders a war between the Community's Member States impossible. More than 40 years of peace in Europe are proof of this.

Unity as the Community's leitmotiv

Unity is the Community's leitmotiv. Present-day problems can be mastered only if the European countries move forward along the path that leads them to unity. Many people take the view that without European integration, without the European Community, it would not be possible to secure peace both in Europe and in the world, democracy, law and justice, economic prosperity and social security and guarantee them for the future. Unemployment, inflation and inadequate growth have long ceased to be merely national problems; nor can they be resolved at national level. It is only in the context of the Community that a stable economic order can be established and only through joint European efforts that an international economic policy can be secured that improves the performance of the European economy and contributes to social justice.

Without internal cohesion, Europe cannot assert its political and economic independence from the rest of the world, win back its influence in the world and retrieve its role in world politics.

Equality must be the rule

Unity can endure only where equality is the rule. This means equality not only as between citizens of the Community but also as between the Member States. No citizen of the Community may be placed at a disadvantage or discriminated against because of his nationality. All Community citizens are equal before the law. As far as the Member States are concerned, the principle of equality means that no State has precedence over another and natural differences such as size, population and differing structures must be dealt with only in accordance with the principle of equality.

The fundamental freedoms

Freedom results directly from peace, unity and equality. Creating a larger entity by linking 12 States immediately affords freedom of movement beyond national frontiers. This means, in particular, freedom of movement for workers, freedom of establishment, freedom to provide services, free movement of goods and freedom of capital movements and payments. These fundamental freedoms, as they are called, under the founding treaties guarantee businessmen freedom of decision-making, workers freedom to choose their place of work and consumers freedom of choice between the greatest possible variety of products. Freedom of competition permits businessmen to offer their goods and services to an incomparably wider circle of potential customers. Workers can seek employment and change their place of employment according to their own ideas and interests throughout the entire territory of the Community. Consumers can select the cheapest and best products from the far greater wealth of goods on offer that results from increased competition.

The principle of solidarity

Solidarity is the necessary corrective to freedom, for ruthless exercise of freedom is always at the expense of others. For this reason, if a Community framework is to continue to endure, it must also always recognize the solidarity of its members as a fundamental principle, and share both the advantages, i.e. prosperity, and the burdens equally and justly among its members.

The need for security

Lastly, all these fundamental values are dependent upon security. In the most recent past, particularly, a period characterized by movement and change, and by the totally unknown, security has become a basic need which the Community must also endeavour to satisfy. Every action by Community institutions must pay heed to the need to render the future predictable for Community citizens and firms and to lend permanence to the circumstances upon which they are dependent. This is the case not only as regards job security but also as regards business decisions

taken in reliance on the continuance of existing general economic conditions and, lastly, the social security of citizens of the Community.

Fundamental rights in the Community

Once reference has been made to fundamental values and the concepts that underlie them, the question necessarily arises of the fundamental rights of individual citizens of the Community. This is particularly so, since the history of Europe has, for more than 200 years, been characterized by continuing efforts to strengthen the protection of fundamental rights. Starting with the declarations of human and civil rights in the 18th century, fundamental rights and civil liberties are firmly anchored in the constitutions of most civilized States. This is especially true of the Member States of the European Community, whose legal systems are constructed on the basis of observance of the law and respect for the dignity, freedom and the right to self-development of the individual. There are, moreover, numerous international conventions concerning the protection of human rights, among which the European Convention for the Protection of Human Rights and Fundamental Freedoms, of 4 November 1950, is of very great significance. At the Helsinki Conference on Security and Cooperation in Europe (CSCE) the protection of human rights was among the most important demands made by Western countries.

A search through the Community treaties for express provisions concerning the fundamental rights of individual Community citizens is disappointing. In contrast to the legal systems of the Member States, the Community treaties contain neither a list of fundamental rights nor any generally binding commitment to respect and protect the fundamental rights and freedoms of Community citizens as, for example, was laid down in the European Defence Community Treaty of 27 May 1952. The Community treaties do not even mention the terms 'fundamental right' or 'human rights'.

Why are the treaties silent on this matter? Does the EC have no regard for fundamental rights? Is it not concerned to meet the basic obligation to secure the legal rights of the individual?

The answer is emphatically no!

If one gives up looking for express guarantees of fundamental rights, one finds that there are provisions scattered throughout the treaty texts whose content is intended to protect Community citizens and which are very similar to certain of the Member States' guarantees of fundamental rights.

This is especially the case as far as the numerous prohibitions on discrimination are concerned which, in specific circumstances, express particular aspects of the general principle of equality. Examples are to be found in Article 6 of the EC Treaty* concerning the prohibition of any discrimination on grounds of nationality, Articles 48, 52 and 60 of the EC Treaty on equal treatment of Community citizens in regard to the right to work, freedom of establishment and freedom to provide services, Article 85 *et seq.* of the EC Treaty on freedom of competition, and Article 119 of the EC Treaty concerning equal pay for men and women.

The Community rules that establish the four fundamental freedoms of the Community, which guarantee the fundamental freedoms of professional life, can be regarded as constituting a Community fundamental right to freedom of movement and freedom to choose and practise a profession. The rules in question are those relating to the freedom of movement of workers (Article 48 EC), the right of establishment (Article 52 EC) and freedom to provide services (Article 59 EC) and freedom of movement of goods (Article 9 *et seq.* EC).

---

* Formerly Article 7 of the EEC Treaty.

Lastly, other spheres of fundamental rights are recognized in individual provisions of the Community treaties. Those of particular significance here are the right of association (Article 118(1) EC and the first paragraph of Article 48 ECSC), the right to submit comments (second paragraph of Article 48 ECSC) and the protection of business and professional secrets (Article 214 EC, Article 194 Euratom and the second and fourth paragraphs of Article 47 ECSC).

Although in the case-law of the early years, the Court of Justice of the European Communities did not regard the application of fundamental rights within the Community as an issue with which it had to concern itself, since 1969 it has continually developed and added to these initial attempts at protecting the fundamental rights of Community citizens. The starting point in this case law was the *Stauder* judgment, in which the point at issue was the fact that a recipient of

welfare benefits for war victims regarded the requirement that he give his name when registering for the purchase of butter at reduced prices at Christmas time as a violation of his human dignity and the principle of equality. Although the Court of Justice came to the conclusion, in interpreting the Community provision, that it was not necessary for recipients to give their name so that, in fact, consideration of the question of a violation of a fundamental right was superfluous, it declared finally that the general fundamental principles of the Community legal order, which the Court of Justice has to safeguard, include respect for fundamental rights. This was the first time that the Court of Justice recognized the existence of a Community framework of fundamental rights of its own. In later judgments the Court of Justice then made clear the criteria according to which it intended to ensure protection of fundamental rights at Community level. These are, firstly, the concepts that are common to the constitutions of the Member States and, secondly, the international conventions concerning the protection of human rights to whose conclusion the Member States have been party or to which they have acceded. The Court of Justice has gradually recognized a number of fundamental rights on this basis and has incorporated them into the Community legal order. The EC being directed primarily towards economic objectives, the thrust of rights protection was inevitably both economic and social. In the 1970s, rights of ownership and freedom to engage in an occupation, with the concomitant freedom to engage in business and the right to work, were at the forefront. Cases concerning them arose chiefly from the rules and regulations on the organization of agricultural markets. Later they were joined by freedom of assembly and association, freedom of opinion and religious freedoms (notably in disputes relating to the European public service), respect for privacy and familiy life (notably in connection with family members' rights to join a migrant worker), confidentiality of correspondence between lawyer and client (privileged communications, as they are known in the common law countries), and the inviolability of residential accommodation (out of bounds to Commission antitrust investigators). One particularly important principle, regularly invoked in disputes with the Community, is the principle of equal treatment. Put simply, this means that like cases must be treated alike, unless there is some objectively justifiable ground for distinguishing them. But the Court of Justice has held, contrary to international custom, that this principle does not preclude nationals and home-produced goods from being subjected to stricter requirements than citizens or products from other Member States. This reverse discrimination, as it is known, is the inevitable result of the limited scope of the Community's powers. The Community rules requiring liberalization, which flow from the fundamental Community freedoms, apply by the Court's definition only to cross-border trade. Rules regulating the production and marketing of home-produced goods or the legal status of nationals within their Member State are affected by Community law only if the Community has taken harmonization measures.

It is doubtful, to put it mildly, whether the Court's principle will remain valid following the changed — i.e. extended — objectives of the Community since the internal market was completed on 1 January 1993. For one thing, Article 7a EC* defines the internal market as 'an area without internal frontiers in which the free movement of goods, persons, services and capital is ensured in accordance with the provisions of this Treaty'. The Court of Justice will in the near future have to consider whether purely domestic circumstances can be excluded from the operation of the Treaty in this new internal market situation. There is also the question of the value of the statement by the Heads of State or Government relating to Article 7a that the determination of the 31 December 1992

---

* Formerly Article 8a EEC.

deadline for completion of the internal market is not legally binding. Precedents regarding domestic circumstances and reverse discrimination can be reviewed only if the extended objectives of the internal market are acknowledged to be legally binding.

The cases decided by the Court of Justice have given the Community an extensive body of quasi-constitutional law. In practical terms the principle of proportionality is foremost among these. What it means is that the objectives pursued and the means deployed must be weighed up and an attempt must be made to keep them in proper balance so that the citizen is not subjected to excessive burdens.

Among the other fundamental principles underlying Community law are the general principles of administrative law and the concept of due process: confidentiality must be preserved, retroactive provisions imposing burdens or withdrawing legitimately acquired advantages are precluded and the right to a proper hearing — natural justice is the traditional term for this — must be secured in the administrative procedures of the Commission and the judicial procedures of the Court of Justice.

The European Parliament, the Council and the Commission responded to the Court's decisions by solemnly issuing a Joint Declaration on fundamental rights on 5 April 1977. They underscored the importance of securing these rights in the Community and undertook to preserve them in the exercices of their powers and in the pursuit of the Community's objectives. At the Copenhagen European Council on 7 and 8 April 1978 the Heads of State or Government of the Member States issued a declaration on democracy in which they endorsed the 1977 Declaration. The two declarations may not generate directly exercisable rigths for the Community's citizens, but they are of great political significance as evidence of the status accorded to human rights in the Community.

With all due recognition of the achievements of the Court of Justice in the development of unwritten fundamental rights, this process of deriving 'European fundamental rights' has a serious disadvantage: the Court of Justice is confined to the particular case in point. The result of this can be that it is not able to develop fundamental rights from the general legal principles for all areas in which this appears necessary or desirable. Nor will it be able to elaborate the scope of and the limits to the protection of fundamental rights as generally and distinctively as is necessary. As a result, the Community institutions cannot assess sufficiently precisely whether they are in danger of violating a fundamental right or not. Nor can any Community citizen who is affected judge in every case whether one of his fundamental rights has been infringed. The resultant uncertainty in the law can ultimately be cleared up only by a Community Bill of Rights. But this would entail amending the existing treaties, which in turn entails the consensus of the Member States on the scope and substance of the rights to be secured. That consensus has not yet emerged. Both in the Single European Act and in the Treaty on European Union, the Member States were unable to agree on anything more than a vague compromise formulation to the effect that the EC would respect the rights secured by the European Convention on Human Rights and the general principles of Community law flowing from their common constitutional traditions.

■ THE INSTITUTIONS OF THE COMMUNITY

The third question arising in connection with the constitution of the European Community is that of its organization. What are the institutions of the Community? Since the Community exercises functions normally reserved for States, does it have a government, a parliament, administrative authorities and courts like those with which we are familiar in the Member States?

Action on the tasks assigned to the Community and the direction of the integration process were intentionally not left in the hands of the Member States or of pure international cooperation. The EC has an institutional system that equips it to give new stimuli and objectives to the unification of Europe and to create a body of Community law that is uniformly devised and applied in relevant matters in all the Member States.

The main actors on the Community stage are the European Council, in a class of its own, and the institutions strictly so called — the European Parliament, the Council (sometimes known as the Council of Ministers), the Commission, the Court of Justice and, following entry into force of the Maastricht Treaty, the Court of Auditors. There are also a number of ancillary bodies.

Of these institutions the Court of Justice and Parliament, or Assembly as it used to be called, were from the outset common to the three Communities. This was provided for in a Convention between the original six Member States that was signed in 1957 at the same time as the Rome Treaties. The process of creating common institutions was completed in July 1967 by the Treaty establishing a Single Council and a Single Commission of the European Communities (the 'Merger Treaty'). Since then all three Communities have had one and the same institutional structure.

The European Council (Article 2 of the Single European Act)

The European Council was created out of the Summit Conferences of Heads of State or Government. At the Paris Summit on 9 and 10 December 1974 it was decided that meetings should be held three times a year and described as the European Council. In 1987 Article 2 of the Single Act formally incorporated it in the Community's institutional set-up.

The Heads of State or Government and the President of the Commission meet at least twice a year in this context. They are accompanied by the Foreign Ministers and a Member of the Commission (Single Act, Article 2).

The function of the European Council is to establish policy guidelines for European integration in terms both of the Community as such and of political cooperation. In the Community context it does so by taking basic policy decisions and issuing instructions and guidelines to the Council or the Representatives of the Member States meeting in the Council. The European Council has in this way directed work on economic and monetary union, the European Monetary System, direct elections to Parliament and a number of accession applications. Community legislation can also be enacted, and the European Council would then be acting as the Council of the Communities; but this has never yet happened in fact. The European Council's functions in the context of political cooperation consist largely of agreeing opinions on questions of international relations and the coordination of the Member States' foreign policies.

The European Parliament (Articles 137 *et seq.* EC)

The European Parliament represents the peoples of the Member States of the Community.

Before 1979 Members of the European Parliament were selected from the membership of national parliaments and delegated by them. The direct general election of MEPs by the peoples of the Member States was provided for in the treaties themselves, but the first direct elections were not held until June 1979, a number of earlier initiatives having been fruitless. Elections are now held every five years, but there is still no uniform electoral procedure as required by the treaties: national systems continued to apply even at the third election in 1989. The United Kingdom maintained its 'first-past-the-post' system for European as for national elections, whereas all the other Member States applied proportional representation systems.

The composition of Parliament is shown in graphic form below; this is the situation following the 1989 elections. The number of seats is to be raised to 567 for the 1994 elections to reflect the position in Germany following the merger of the two separate German states that existed earlier. People living in the five new *Länder* must now be represented, and the number of German MEPs is to rise by 18, from 81 to 99. For the current legislature their 18 representatives enjoy observer status. The number of MEPs representing the other Member States is also to be adjusted. France, Italy and the UK will have 87 each instead of 81, Spain will have 64 (60), the Netherlands 31 (25), and Belgium, Greece and Portugal 25 (24). The representation of Denmark (16), Ireland (15) and Luxembourg (6) remains unchanged.

Now that it is directly elected, Parliament can truly claim to represent the peoples of the Community; it enjoys democratic legitimacy. But the mere existence of a directly elected Parliament cannot satisfy the fundamental requirement of a democratic constitution that all public authority must emanate from the people. That calls not only for transparency of the decision-making process but also for representativeness in the decision-making institutions and the involvement of those concerned. It is precisely in this respect that the current organization of the Community leaves something to be desired. It is therefore rightly described as a still underdeveloped democracy. The European Parliament exercises only symbolically the functions of a true parliament such as exists in a parliamentary democracy. Firstly, Parliament does not elect a government. This is simply because no government in the normal sense exists at Community level. Instead, the functions analogous to government provided for in the treaties are performed by the Council and the Commission according to a form of division of labour. Admittedly, the Treaty on European Union now gives Parliament power to influence the Commission's membership through the appointment procedure. The Commission President is appointed by the Governments of the Member States only after Parliament has been consulted, and both the President and the other Members are then subject as a body to a vote of approval in Parliament. But Parliament has no influence over the membership of the Council. The Council is subject to parliamentary control only in so far as each of its members, as a national minister, is answerable to the national parliament. Parliament's actual functions are described below.

Advisory functions. Parliament exercises advisory functions primarily through the treaty provisions requiring it to be consulted. These secure its role in the EC legislative process in the many cases where its opinion must be sought on a Commission proposal before the Council decides on it (mandatory consultation). But Parliament's influence over the Council's ultimate decision is somewhat tenuous since the Council is not bound to heed Parliament's views. It is stronger where the Commission defends Parliament's position in relations with the Council. There has been an extension of Parliament's influence, at least in quantitative terms, in that the new

EUROPEAN PARLIAMENT: 518 Members
(567 Members from June 1994)

Parliament is presided over by a President assisted by 14 Vice-Presidents

- Group of the Party of European Socialists — 198
- Group of the European People's Party (Christian Democratic Group) — 163
- Liberal Democratic and Reformist Group — 44
- The Green Group in the European Parliament — 28
- Group of the European Democratic Alliance — 20
- Rainbow Group in the European Parliament — 16
- Technical Group of the European Right — 14
- Left Unity Group — 13
- Non-attached — 22

518

19 committees prepare the work of the plenary sessions

B	DK	D	GR	E	F	IRL	I	L	NL	P	UK
24	16	81	24	60	81	15	81	6	25	24	81

Political composition of the European Parliament (situation on 21 June 1993)

Composition of the European Parliament
(Situation at 21 June 1993)

1	Group of the Party of European Socialists	198 Members
2	Group of the European People's Party	163 Members
3	Liberal, Democratic and Reformist Group	44 Members
4	The Green Group in the European Parliament	28 Members
5	Group of the European Democratic Alliance	20 Members
6	Rainbow Group in the European Parliament	16 Members
7	Technical Group of the European Right	14 Members
8	Left Unity Group	13 Members
9	Non-attached	22 Members

1. Committee on Foreign Affairs and Security

2. Committee on Agriculture, Fisheries and Rural Development

3. Committee on Budgets

4. Committee on Economic and Monetary Affairs and Industrial Policy

5. Committee on Energy, Research and Technology

6. Committee on External Economic Relations

7. Committee on Legal Affairs and Citizens' Rights

8. Committee on Social Affairs, Employment and the Working Environment

9. Committee on Regional Policy and Relations with Regional and Local Authorities

10. Committee on Transport and Tourism

11. Committee on the Environment, Public Health and Consumer Protection

12. Committee on Culture, Youth, Education and the Media

13. Committee on Development and Cooperation

14. Committee on Civil Liberties and Internal Affairs

15. Committee on Budgetary Control

16. Committee on Institutional Affairs

17. Committee on the Rules of Procedure, the Verification of Credentials and Immunities

18. Committee on Women's Rights

19. Committee on Petitions

procedures provide for the possibility of consulting it even in those matters where consultation is not obligatory (optional consultation). The cooperation procedure, introduced for all decisions of any moment for the internal market, has considerably strengthened Parliament's arm in the decision-making process. This procedure will be considered in more detail in the section on the EC legislation process; the most striking innovation is that there is now a second reading stage in Parliament.

Supervisory functions. Parliament has supervisory powers only over the Commission. They are exercised mainly through the fact that the Commission must answer parliamentary questions, must defend its proposals before it and must present it with an annual report on the activities of the Communities for debate. Parliament can by a two-thirds majority of its members pass a motion of censure and thereby compel the Commission to resign as a body. Four motions of censure have so far been tabled; only two of them came to the vote (in 1976), and they were lost. Since in practice the Council also answers parliamentary questions, Parliament has the opportunity for direct political debate with the two lawmaking institutions and has in fact made extensive use of it. The Treaty on European Union substantially boosts Parliament's supervisory powers. Apart from its role in the Commission's appointment, it is now empowered to set up special Committees of Inquiry to investigate

THE COUNCIL

**Representatives
of the governments
of the Member States
12**

**Permanent
Representatives
Committee
(Coreper)**

Legislation

Weighting of votes

10	France
10	Germany
10	Italy
10	United Kingdom
8	Spain
5	Portugal

Weighting of votes

Greece	5
Netherlands	5
Belgium	5
Denmark	3
Ireland	3
Luxembourg	2

Qualified majority:
54 votes out of 76

alleged cases of maladministration or infringement of Community law which are not the subject of judicial proceedings. Its right to receive and examine petitions has also been written into the treaties, together with the power to appoint an Ombudsman.

Decision-making functions. Since 1975 Parliament can claim to have had a special status in the budgetary field. It establishes the budget in conjunction with the Council and, subject to certain conditions and in certain categories of expenditure, has the power to make amendments which even the Council cannot oppose; in other words, it has the last say. The Single European Act gave it a substantial say on a number of other matters, in that decisions to accept new Member States and to associate non-member countries require its assent. The Treaty on European Union extended the scope of the assent procedure to new areas. They include the decision on a uniform electoral procedure, the Structural Funds Regulations, the conclusion of international treaties and several key decisions required for economic and monetary union, such as the constitution and responsibilities of the European Central Bank. And the new co-decision procedure further strengthens its role in the EC legislative process. Here it has its right of veto and is no longer confined, as it was under the cooperation procedure, to voting against a proposal and thus merely making it more difficult for the Council to take the decision. By threatening the veto, Parliament can now induce the Council to refrain from passing the planned measure. The details of these procedures will again be considered in greater detail in the section on the Community legislative process.

This extension of its powers gives grounds for expecting that Parliament will acquire further true decision-making powers in future. The history of the parliamentary system of government shows that in the 19th century parliaments were first vested with budgetary powers before becoming, sometimes after a hard struggle, the legislative organ.

'It was a stroke of genius on the part of the authors of the Treaty to have invented the Commission, not only because of its right of initiative but also because of this collective memory factor. Without it there can be no continuity.'

Jacques Delors, *A Tribute to Emile Noël, (1987)* p. 67

'We cannot simplify the questions about Europe.
But we must simplify the answers.'

Pierre Uri, *Libération,* 7 June 1989

'The Treaty strikes an overall balance:
the sum of the sacrifices made by any of the parties is offset by the sum of the advantages gained'.

Walter Hallstein, *Die Europäische Gemeinschaft* (Fifth edition), p. 9

The Council (Articles 145 *et seq.* EC)

The Council is made up of representatives of the governments of the Member States. All 12 Member States send one or more representatives — as a rule, though not necessarily, the departmental or junior minister responsible for the matters under consideration, such as the Minister for Foreign Affairs, Economic Affairs, Finance, Labour, Agriculture, Transport or Technology.

It is in the Council that the individual interests of the Member States and the Community interest are balanced and reconciled.

Although the Member States' interests are given precedence in the Council, the members of the Council are at the same time obliged to take into account the objectives and needs of the European Community as a whole. The Council is a Community institution and not an intergovernmental conference. Consequently it is not the lowest common denominator between the Member States that is sought in the Council's deliberations, but the highest between the Community and the Member States. The Council is assisted by a Permanent Representatives Committee (known as Coreper, a contraction of its French title, Comité des représentants permanents). Coreper's members are officials of the Member States with ambassador rank. It prepares the ground for the Council's deliberations and performs the tasks assigned to it by the Council. It plays a vital role in the Council's decision-making process. If it reaches full agreement on a proposed piece of Community legislation, the item is entered on the Council's agenda as an A item, meaning that the Council need do no more than formally record its approval without further debate. Only such items as cannot be dealt with in this way appear on the Council's agenda as B items, for dicussion of outstanding issues and differences of opinion.

In the case of the two more recent Communities, the Council is the supreme legislative body. It takes the most important political decisions of the Community. With regard to the ECSC, on the other hand, it is an endorsing body that has to deal only with a few, especially important decisions.

Under the Community treaties, majority voting in the Council is the rule. The EC Treaty provides for unanimity only in areas of political sensitivity for the Member States such as the social security of workers or taxation and in the implementation of the special 'stop-gap' powers under Article 235. Where no express provision is made to the contrary, a simple majority suffices, and each State has one vote. Normally, however, a 'qualified' majority is required, where votes are weighted so that the larger States exert a greater influence. Thus, France, the Federal Republic of Germany, Italy and the United Kingdom each have 10 votes, Spain eight votes, the Netherlands, Belgium, Greece and Portugal five votes, Denmark and Ireland three votes and Luxembourg two votes. The importance of majority voting lies not so much in the fact that it prevents small States from blocking important decisions, as such members could as a rule be brought into line by political pressure. What the majority principle does is make it possible to outvote large Member States that would withstand political pressure. This principle thus contributes to the equality of Member States and must therefore be regarded as a cornerstone of the Community constitution. For a long time, despite this original and intrinsically well-balanced approach, the importance of the majority principle in practice remained small. The reason for this dates back to 1965 when France, afraid that its vital interests in the financing of the common agricultural policy were threatened, blocked decision-making in the Council for more than six months by a 'policy of the empty chair'.

It was not until 29 January 1966 that this dispute was resolved by the 'Luxembourg Agreement', which states that in the case of decisions where very important interests of one or more countries are at stake, the Council will endeavour, within a reasonable time, to reach solutions that can be adopted by all the members of the Council while respecting their mutual interests and those of the Community. The French delegation emphasized that it considered that in these cases the discussion must be continued until 'unanimous agreement' was reached. The Luxembourg Agreement provides no solution for cases where reaching unanimity proves impossible, but confines itself to stating that a divergence of views on this point still exists among the Member States. This Agreement did succeed in putting an end to the deadlock in the Council, but it also in practice spelt an end to the majority principle. It provides no criteria for determining within the Council whether very important interests are in fact at stake. It is left purely to the Member State concerned to decide this, so that in effect any Member State can demand unanimity for any major decision in the Council. Thus, each Member State has in practice a right of veto. This situation, which detracted from the decision-making ability

THE EUROPEAN COMMISSION

1 President
6 Vice-Presidents
7 Members

Members			Members
1	Belgium	Italy	2
1	Denmark	Luxembourg	1
2	France	Netherlands	1
2	Germany	Portugal	1
1	Greece	Spain	2
1	Ireland	United Kingdom	2

Responsibilities

| **Proposing** measures for the further development of Community policy | **Monitoring** observance and proper application of Community law | **Administering** and implementing Community legislation | **Representing** the Community in international organizations |

of the Council, has been considerably improved by the Single European Act. Although it was not possible to abolish the unanimity rule altogether, it was agreed to give greater emphasis to majority voting — for example, on measures to harmonize legislative and administrative provisions concerning the establishment and functioning of the internal market, economic and social cohesion, research and technological development and the environment. However, exceptions to the majority voting rule were made in the case of taxation, the free movement of labour and the rights and interests of workers, areas where unanimity is still required.

The Commission
(Articles 155 *et seq.* EC)

Since the accession of Greece, Portugal and Spain, the Commission has consisted of 17 members (two members each from France, Germany, Italy, Spain and the United Kingdom, and one from each of the other Member States) appointed hitherto by 'common accord' of the governments of the Member States for a term of four years. Here Parliament's role in appointing the Commission by virtue of the Treaty on European Union, to which we have already referred, has changed the old procedures quite considerably, in that the governments of the Member States must seek Parliament's opinion on any person they are envisaging appointing as Commission President. In agreement with the President-designate they then designate the other members of the Commission. Parliament then votes to approve (or not) the President and Members as a body; if it does so, they are appointed by agreement between the governments of the Member States for a five-year term. This extension from four to five years is to make the Commission's term coincide with the life of a Parliament.

The Commission's functions may be broken down as follows:

(i) The Commission is first of all the motive power behind Community policy. It is the starting point for every Community action, as it is the Commission that has to present proposals and drafts for Community legislation to the Council (this is termed the Commission's right of initiative). The Commission is not free to choose its own activities. It is obliged to act if the Community interest so requires. The Council and, under the Treaty on European Union, Parliament may also ask the Commission to draw up a proposal. Under the ECSC Treaty, however, the Commission also has lawmaking powers. In certain circumstances these are subject to the assent of the Council, which enables it to overrule Commission measures.

(ii) The Commission is also the guardian of the Community treaties. It sees to it that the treaty provisions and the measures adopted by the Community institutions are properly implemented. Whenever they are infringed the Commission must intervene as an impartial body and, if necessary, refer the matter to the Court of Justice. The Commission has so far performed this role very effectively.

(iii) Closely connected with the role of guardian is the task of defending the Community's interests. As a matter of principle, the Commission may serve no interests other than those of the Community. It must constantly endeavour, in what often prove to be difficult negotiations within the Council, to make the Community interest prevail and seek compromise solutions that take account of that interest. In so doing, it also plays the role of mediator between the Member States, a role for which, by virtue of its neutrality, it is particularly suited and qualified.

(iv) Lastly, the Commission is — albeit to a limited extent — an executive body. Classic examples of this are the implementation of the Community budget, competition law and the administration of the protective clauses contained in the treaties and secondary legislation. The Commission has been given a crucial role to play in its executive capacity in the preparation of economic and monetary union. It is responsible for overseeing and directing policy on convergence in the run-up to the third stage of monetary union, it is to be represented at meetings of the Governing Council of the European Central Bank and it is to represent the Community and speak for it in international monetary relations. Much more extensive than these 'primary' executive powers are the 'derived' powers devolved on the Commission by the Council. These essentially involve adopting the requisite detailed rules for implementing Council decisions. As a rule, however, it is the Member States themselves that have to ensure that Community rules are applied in individual cases. This solution chosen by the treaties has the advantage that citizens are brought closer to what is still to them the 'foreign' reality of the European system through the workings and in the familiar form of the national system.

The Court of Justice (Articles 164 *et seq.* EC)

A system will endure only if its rules are supervised by an independent authority. What is more, in a community of States the common rules — if they are subject to control by the national courts — are interpreted and applied differently from one State to another. The uniform application of Community law in all Member States would thus be jeopardized. These considerations led to the establishment of a Community Court of Justice as soon as the ECSC was created.

Since Greece, Portugal and Spain became members of the Communities, the Court of Justice has consisted of 13 judges, appointed by common accord of the governments of the Member States for a renewable term of six years.

Members are chosen from persons whose independence is beyond doubt and who possess the qualifications required for appointment to the highest judicial offices in their respective countries or who are jurisconsults of recognized competence. The Court is assisted by six Advocates-General whose term of office corresponds to that of the judges; they enjoy judicial independence. The submissions of the Advocates-General provide a full survey of all the questions of law raised in the case before the Court together with a proposal for the decision to be reached by the Court.

The function of the Court of Justice is to ensure that in the interpretation and application of the Treaties and of instruments enacted under them the law is observed. In exercising that function it operates in matters that in the Member States would be assigned to different types of court, depending on their national systems. It acts as a constitutional court when disputes between Community institutions are before it or legislative instruments are up for review for legality; as an administrative court when reviewing the administrative acts of the Commission or of national authorities applying Community legislation; as a labour court or industrial tribunal when dealing with freedom of movement, social security and equal opportunities; as a criminal court when reviewing Commission decisions imposing fines; and as a civil court when hearing claims for damages or interpreting the Brussels Convention on the Enforcement of Judgments in Civil and Commercial Matters.

From the outset the Court of Justice has never seen its role as confined to dispute settlement: it regards itself as a body of creative lawmakers. It is to its credit that it has defined the principles on which the Community legal order rests, thereby providing the process of European integration with a firm foundation. It has been described as an integration factor of the highest order. In its judgments it has broadly followed the rules of interpretation common to the legal systems of the Member States, though it has adapted them to the specific character of the Community legal order and thus produced in effect its own interpretation rules. The literal interpretation rule, which usually ranks first in the Member States, is only of limited value in the Community law context. Community legislation is often not drafted in such a way as to allow the Court to interpret the words strictly, since it is commonly the result of a compromise in the decision-making and the imprecise language used reflects that constraint; moreover, the legislation is binding in nine different language versions, and that further complicates the interpretation. So the Court regularly has to look beyond the strict words used and interpret legislation in the light of its purpose — the teleological technique — to correct these defects. To ascertain the purpose of an instrument, it will often have regard to the objectives of the treaty on which it is based. A number of themes run through its interpretations, such as the principles of equality (no overt or covert discrimination is tolerated), the four freedoms (free movement of goods, persons, services and capital), solidarity (between Member States) and unity (in legal and economic terms).

Under the Single European Act, the Council was empowered to set up, by a unanimous decision, a Court of First Instance to be responsible for dealing with certain classes of action. On 24 October 1988 the Council availed itself of this possibility and adopted a decision setting up such a Court. It consists of 12 members who, in accordance with the

THE EUROPEAN COURT OF JUSTICE

Governments of the
Member States appoint
**the 13 judges
and six Advocates-General**
by common accord for
a term of six years

COURT OF JUSTICE
Full court of 13 judges
2 chambers with 5 judges
4 chambers with 3 judges

TYPES OF PROCEEDING

Actions for failure to fulfil obligations under the Treaties (Commission or Member State v Member State)

Actions for annulment (against Council or Commission)

Actions on grounds of failure to act (against Council or Commission)

Claims for damages against the Community

References from national courts for preliminary rulings to clarify the meaning and scope of Community law

Opinions

COURT OF FIRST INSTANCE
12 judges

Direct actions by natural and legal persons, except anti-dumping cases
Staff cases
Actions under the ECSC Treaty
Ancillary actions for damages

rules of procedure, may also be called on to perform the task of an Advocate-General.

The Court of First Instance has jurisdiction in actions relating to the Staff Regulations of the European Communities, competition law, coal and steel disputes and, under a Council Decision effective on 1 August 1993, all direct actions by citizens and firms against the Community institutions except in anti-dumping matters.

The various types of proceeding are described in more detail in the section on the Community system of legal protection.

Community law lives only in the judgments of the Court. Its judgments convey a feeling of the justness of European law and hence give it the necessary authority *vis-à-vis* governments, government agencies, parliaments and citizens.

The Court of Auditors
(Articles 188a to 188c EC)

The European Court of Auditors was set up by the Treaty of 22 July 1975 and began work in Luxembourg in 1977. It consists of 12 Members, in line with the present number of Member States; they are appointed for six years by the Council following consultation of the European Parliament. Its task is to examine whether all revenue has been received and all expenditure incurred in a lawful and regular manner and whether financial management has been sound. Unlike the courts of auditors or similar bodies in the Member States, it has no jurisdiction to enforce its control measures or to investigate suspicions of irregularity arising from its examination. But is is wholly autonomous in its decisions regarding what it examines and how. It can, for instance, examine whether the use made of Community financial support by private individuals is in conformity with Community law. The chief weapon in its armoury is the fact that it can publicize its findings: the results of its activity are summarized in an annual report at the end of each financial year, which is published in the *Official Journal of the European Communities* and thus brought to public attention. It may also make special reports on specific areas of financial management, and these are published likewise.

Ancillary bodies

In addition to the abovementioned institutions proper there are a number of ancillary bodies. The most important of these, because it is vested with general powers, is the Economic and Social Committee. The Economic and Social Committee advises the Council and Commission on economic matters. It is a forum for such economic and social categories as manufacturers, farmers, carriers, employees, businessmen, small tradesmen and the professions. Because of its composition and its political and technical terms of reference, it exerts a strong influence on the Community's decision-making process. Through its opinions, not only does it provide valuable assistance to those responsible for formulating Community policies, but it also forms a link between the various occupational groups, which ultimately feel directly the practical effects of Community measures, and the European reality. A new advisory body was set up alongside the Economic and Social Committee by the Treaty on European Union — the Committee of the Regions. Like the Economic and Social Committee it is not strictly a Community institution, as its function is purely advisory and it has no power to produce mandatory decisions in the same way that the fully fledged institutions (Parliament, Council, Commission, Court of Justice) do. The Committee of the Regions consists of representatives of regional and local authorities in the Member States, appointed by the Council in proportion to the weightings given the Member States. There are seven areas in which consultation by the Council or the Commission, as the case may be, is mandatory — education, cultural 'incentive measures', public health, the report on economic and social cohesion, basic rules governing all the Structural Funds and implementing rules for the Regional Fund.

As financing agency for a 'balanced and steady development' of the common market, the Community has at its disposal the European Investment Bank (Articles 198d and 198e EC)*. This provides loans and guarantees in all economic sectors to promote the development of less-developed regions, to modernize or convert undertakings or create new jobs and to assist projects of common interest to several Member States.

---

* Formerly Articles 129 and 130 EEC.

THE COMMUNITY AS A LEGAL REALITY

The constitution of the European Community described above, and particularly the fundamental values it establishes, can be brought to life and given substance only through Community law. This makes the Community a legal reality in two different senses: it is created by law and it forms a legal order.

■ THE COMMUNITY IS CREATED BY LAW

This is what is entirely new about the Community, what distinguishes it from earlier efforts to unite Europe. It works not by means of force or domination but simply by means of law. Law is to do what 'blood and iron' have for centuries failed to do. For only unity

SOURCES OF COMMUNITY LAW

Treaty law

Primary legislation
(Treaties
establishing the Communities,
Annexes and Protocols,
amendments to the Treaties,
Treaties of Accession)

General principles of law, customary law

International agreements

Secondary legislation

Regulations and implementing
regulations
Directives/ECSC Recommendations
General and individual decisions

Conventions between the Member States

Decisions of the representatives of the Member States
meeting within the Council

Conventions creating uniform Community law

---

based on a freely made decision can be expected to last: unity founded on the fundamental values such as freedom and equality, and protected and translated into reality by law. That is the insight underlying the treaties that created the Community.

■ THE COMMUNITY IS A LEGAL ORDER

The Community is a legal order, since it is not merely a creation of law but also pursues its objectives purely by means of law. To put it briefly, it is a Community based on law. The common economic and social life of the peoples of the Member States is governed not by the threat of force but by the law of the Community. This Community law, which in all its ramifications shapes the legal order, is drawn from a variety of sources.

It is the basis of the institutional system. Community law lays down the procedure for decision-making by the Community institutions and regulates their relationship to each other. It provides the institutions with the means — in the shape of regulations, general

ECSC decisions, directives, ECSC recommendations and individual decisions — of enacting legal instruments binding on the Member States and their citizens.

Thus the individual himself becomes a main focus of the Community. Its legal order directly affects his daily life to an ever-increasing extent. It accords him rights and imposes on him duties, so that as a citizen both of his State and of the Community he is governed by a hierarchy of legal orders — a phenomenon familiar from federal constitutions. Community law also defines the relationship between the Community and the Member States. The Member States must take all appropriate measures to ensure fulfilment of the obligations arising out of the treaties or resulting from action taken by the institutions of the Community. They must facilitate the achievement of the Community's tasks and abstain from any measure that could jeopardize the attainment of the objectives of the treaties.

Apart from this, two fundamental principles govern the Community legal order: the legality of the acts of the Community organs and the legal protection of those subject to Community rules.

■ THE LEGAL SOURCES OF COMMUNITY LAW

The founding treaties as primary source of Community law

The first source of Community law in this sense is provided by the three treaties, with the various annexes and protocols attached to them, and their later additions and amendments: these are the founding acts which we looked at when we discussed the Community's constitution. The founding treaties and instruments amending and supplementing them — chiefly the Single European Act and the Treaty on European Union — contain the basic provisions on the EC's objectives, organization and *modus operandi,* and the bulk of its economic law. They thus set the constitutional framework for the life of the EC, which is to be fleshed out in the Community interest by legislative and administrative action by the Community institutions. The treaties, being legal instruments created direct by the Member States, are known in the jargon as 'primary legislation'.

The Community legal instruments as secondary source of Community law

Law made by the Community institutions in the exercise of the powers conferred on them by the treaties is referred to as secondary legislation, the second great source of Community law. It covers a range of types of legislative act that had to be devised afresh when the Community was set up. It had to be decided first and foremost what forms Community legislation should take and what effects these forms should have. The institutions had to be able to align the disparate economic, social and not least environmental conditions in the various Member States, and do so effectively, i.e. without depending on the goodwill of the Member States, so that the best possible living conditions could be created for all the citizens of the Community; but on the other hand they were not to interfere in the domestic systems of law any more than necessary. The Community legislative system is therefore based on the principle that where the same arrangement, even on points of detail, must apply in all Member States, national arrangements must be replaced by Community legislation; but where this is not necessary, due account must be taken of the existing legal orders in the Member States.

The Community's range of tools

Against this background a range of tools was developed that allowed the Community institutions to work on the national legal systems in varying measures. The most drastic action is the replacement of national rules by Community rules. Then there are Community rules by which the Community institutions act on the Member States' legal

ECSC	EC	Euratom
(Article 14)	(Article 189)	(Article 161)
• Decisions (general)	• Regulations	• Regulations
• Recommendations	• Directives	• Directives
• Decisions (individual)	• Decisions	• Decisions
—	• Recommendations	• Recommendations
• Opinions	• Opinions	• Opinions

systems only indirectly. Thirdly, measures may be taken that affect only a defined or identifiable addressee, in order to deal with a particular case. Lastly, provision was also made for legal acts that have no binding force, either on the Member States or on the citizens of the Community. These basic categories of legal act are to be found in all three Community treaties. There are differences in the actual form they take, and in their titles, between the ECSC Treaty on the one hand and the EC and the Euratom Treaties on the other. The ECSC Treaty makes provision for only three types of legal act — decisions, recommendations and opinions (Article 14 ECSC); the EC and Euratom Treaties provide for five forms — regulations, directives, decisions, recommendations and opinions (Article 189 EC and Article 161 Euratom). The changes in the pattern arose because it was recognized that the forms developed for the ECSC would not adequately meet the needs of the EC and Euratom. The new titles were intended to avoid the conceptual shortcomings in the legal acts provided for in the earlier treaty. It was felt that the distinctions between the two sets of concepts would simply have to be tolerated until the merger of the three Communities, which it was intended should take place at a later date.

But if we look at the range of Community legal instruments in terms of the person to whom they are addressed and their practical effects in the Member States, we can break them down as follows:

Regulations and ECSC general decisions: Community 'laws'

The legal acts that enable the Community institutions to encroach furthest on the domestic legal systems are regulations in the EC and Euratom Treaties, and general decisions in the ECSC Treaty. Two features very unusual in international law mark them out: (i) Their Community character, which means that they lay down the same law throughout the Community, regardless of international borders, and apply in full in all Member States. A Member State has no power to apply a regulation incompletely or to select only those provisions of which it approves as a means of ensuring that an instrument which it opposed at the time of its adoption or which runs counter to its perceived national interest is not given effect. Nor can it set up provisions or practices of domestic law to preclude the mandatory application of a regulation. (ii) Direct applicability, which means that they do not have to be transposed into national law but confer rights or impose duties on the Community citizen in the same way as domestic law. The Member States and their governing institutions and courts are bound directly by Community law and have to comply with it as they have to comply with domestic law. But in spite of all their similarities with the statute law passed in individual Member States they cannot, strictly speaking, be described as the equivalent at European level, as they are not enacted by the European Parliament and thus, from a formal point of view at least, they lack the essential characteristics of legislation of this kind.

The purpose and effects of a regulation, or a general ECSC decision, can be illustrated by means of two examples. For the regulation we can take the field which has from the beginning been dealt with mainly by means of regulations, namely agriculture. The common market extends to agriculture and trade in agricultural products (Article 38(1) EC), as

we have already seen. In the common agricultural market, goods have to be traded not just inside one country in which the same rules apply, but between buyers and sellers in different countries, so that the market can operate smoothly only if common rules are in force throughout the territory of the Community. This requires joint management centrally for the Community as a whole, and the measures needed for the operation of the market have to have direct force in all Member States. Only a regulation has these effects. The purpose and effect of the general ECSC decision is clearly illustrated in the way in which the Commission intervenes in the Community steel market. The crisis that had been smouldering in the European iron and steel industry since 1975 grew in 1980 into the worst crisis since the war. There was a collapse in demand for steel on the Community market and the world market, which led to a substantial fall in prices in the Community even though production costs were rising. European steel producers' financial position worsened so far that it was feared there would be lasting damage to the steel industry. This would have been a major blow to the attainment of the objectives of the ECSC Treaty, set out in Article 3, particularly the improvement of workers' living and working conditions and the achievement of an orderly Community market. This dangerous situation required direct adjustment of steel output, binding on all steel firms, in order to restore the balance between supply and demand on the steel market. The only suitable instrument is the general ECSC decision, as it is the only instrument which ensures that the necessary measures are binding and actually applied in all Member States and by all steel firms alike.

Directives and ECSC recommendations

The EC/Euratom directive, which has the ECSC recommendation as its equivalent, is the most important legislative instrument alongside the regulation. Its purpose is to reconcile the dual objectives of both securing the necessary uniformity of Community law and respecting the diversity of national traditions and structures. What the directive aims for, then, is not the unification of the law, which is the regulation's purpose, but its harmonization. The idea is to remove contradictions and conflicts between national laws and regulations or gradually even out inconsistencies so that as far as possible the same conditions in substance obtain in all the Member States. The directive is one of the primary means deployed in building the single market.

A directive is binding on the Member States as regards the objective to be achieved but leaves to the national authorities the choice of form and methods used to attain the objective agreed on at Community level within their domestic legal systems. The reasoning behind this form of legislation is that it allows intervention in domestic economic and legal structures to take a milder form. In particular, Member States can take account of special domestic circumstances when implementing Community rules. What happens is that the directive does not supersede the laws of the Member States but places the Member States under an obligation to adapt their national law in line with Community rules. The result is a two-stage lawmaking process. First, at the Community stage, the directive lays down the objective that is to be achieved by the Member State or Member States, possibly all of them, to whom it is addressed with a specified time-frame. The Community institutions can actually spell out the objective in such detailed terms as to leave the Member States with scant room for manoeuvre, and this has in fact been done in directives on technical standards and environmental protection. Second, at the national stage, the objective set at Community level is translated into actual legal or administrative provisions in the Member States.

Even if the Member States are in principle free to determine the form and methods used to transpose their Community obligation into domestic law, the assessment of whether they have done so properly in accordance with Community law is made in the light of Community criteria. The general principle is that a legal situation must be generated in which the rights and obligations flowing from the directive can be recognized with adequate clarity and certainty so that the Community citizen can rely on them or challenge them, as the case may be, in the national courts. This broadly means enacting mandatory national rules of law or repealing or amending existing rules.

Apart from cases where ECSC recommendations are addressed direct to a firm, directives and ECSC recommendations addressed to one or more Member States do not as a rule directly confer rights or impose obligations on the Community citizen. They are expressly addressed to the Member States alone. Rights and obligations for the citizen flow only from the measures enacted by the authorities of the Member States to implement the directive or recommendation. This point is of no importance to the citizen as long as the Member States actually comply with their Community obligation. But there are disadvantages for the Community citizen where a Member State does not take the requisite implementing measures to achieve an objective set in a directive or recommendation that would benefit him or where the measures taken are inadequate. The Court of Justice has refused to tolerate such disadvantages, and a long line of cases has determined that in such circumstances the Community citizen can plead the directive or recommendation direct in actions in the national courts to secure the rights conferred on him by it. Direct effect, as it is known, is available only where the provisions of the directive are sufficiently clear and precise, the alleged rights are not conditional, the national authorities were given no room for manoeuvre regarding the content of the rules to be enacted and the time allowed for implementation of the directive has expired.

The decisions of the Court of Justice in direct effect cases are based on the general consideration that the Member State is acting contradictorily and unlawfully if it applies its old law without adapting it to the requirements of the directive or recommendation. This is an abuse of rights by the State and the recognition of direct effect of the directive seeks to combat it by ensuring that the State derives no benefit from its violation of Community law. Direct effect thus has the effect of penalizing the offending Member State. In that context it is significant that the Court of Justice has applied the principle solely in cases between citizen and Member State and then, only when the directive was for the citizen's benefit and not to his detriment, in other words when the citizen's position under the law as amended under the directive was more favourable than under the old law (what is known as vertical direct effect). Direct effect in relations between citizens themselves (horizontal direct effect) has not yet been accepted by the Court of Justice. The Court concludes from the punitive nature of the principle that it is not applicable to relations between private individuals since they cannot be held liable for the consequences of the State's failure to act. What the citizen needs to rely on is certainty in the law and the protection of legitimate expectations. The citizen must be able to count on the effect of a directive being achieved by national implementation measures.

In its judgment in the 1991 cases of *Francovich* and *Bonifaci,* the Court of Justice went further, holding that Member States are liable to pay damages where loss is sustained by reason of failure to transpose a directive in whole or in part. Both cases were brought against Italy for failure to transpose Directive 80/987/EEC on the protection of employees in the event of the employer's insolvency; that Directive sought to protect the employee's rights to remuneration in the period preceding insolvency and dismissal on grounds of insolvency. To that end, guarantee funds were to be established with protection from creditors; they were to be funded by employers, the public authorities or both. The problem facing the Court was that, although the aim of the Directive was to confer on employed workers a personal right to continued payment of remuneration from the guarantee funds, this right could not be given direct effect by the national courts, meaning that they could not enforce it against the national authorities, since in the absence of measures transposing the Directive the guarantee fund had not been established and it was not possible to ascertain who was the debtor in relation to payment of sums related to the insolvency. The Court finally held that by failing to implement the Directive Italy had deprived the employed workers in question of their rights under it and was accordingly liable in damages. Even if the duty to compensate is not written into Community law, the Court of Justice sees it as an integral part of the Community legal order since its full effect would not be secured and the rights conferred by it would not be protected if Community citizens did not have the possibility of seeking and obtaining compensation for invasion of their rights by Member States acting in contravention of Community law.

Individual decisions: the Community's 'administrative measures'

A third category of Community legal acts consists of EC or Euratom decisions and individual ECSC decisions. In some cases the Community institutions may themselves be responsible for implementing the treaties, or regulations and general ECSC decisions, and this will be possible only if they are in a position to take measures binding on particular individuals, firms or Member States. The situation in the Member States' own systems is the same. Legislation will be applied by the authorities in an individual case by means of an administrative decision. In the Community legal order this function is fulfilled by the individual decision. The individual decision is the means normally available to the Community institutions to order something to be done in an individual case. The Community institutions can thus require a Member State or an individual to perform or to refrain from some action, or can confer rights or impose duties on them. The structural features of a decision can be summed up as follows. (i) It is distinguished from the regulation by being of individual application: the persons to whom it is addressed must be named in it and are the only ones bound by it. That requirement is met if at the time the decision is issued the category of addresses can be identified and can thereafter not be extended. Reference is made to the actual content of the decision, which must be such as to have a direct, individual impact on the citizen's situation. Even a third party may be within the definition if by reason of personal qualities or circumstances that distinguish him from others he is individually affected and is identifiable as such in the same way as the addressee. (ii) It is distinguished from the directive in that it is binding in tis entirety (the directive simply sets objectives to be attained). (iii) It is directly applicable to those to whom it is addressed. A decision addressed to a Member State can, incidentally, have the same direct effect in relation to the citizen as a directive.

Recommendations and opinions

Lastly there are opinions and EC and Euratom recommendations. This category of legal measures is the last one explicitly provided for in the treaties; it enables the Community institutions to express a view to Member States, and in some cases to individual citizens, which is not binding and does not place any legal obligation on the addressees. In the EC and Euratom Treaties these non-binding legal measures are called recommendations or opinions, but under the ECSC Treaty only the term opinions is used. Unhappily, in the ECSC system a 'recommendation' is a binding legal act, corresponding to the directive in the EC and Euratom Treaties. In any event, while EC and Euratom recommendations urge the addressees to adopt a particular form of behaviour, opinions are used where the Community institutions are called upon to state a view on a current situation or particular event in the Community or the Member States.

The real significance of these recommendations and opinions is political and moral. In providing for legal acts of this kind the draftsmen of the treaties proceeded on the expectation that, given the prestige of the Community institutions, and their broader view and wide knowledge of conditions beyond the narrower national framework, those concerned would voluntarily comply with recommendations made to them and would draw the appropriate consequences from the Community institutions' assessment of a particular situation.

Recommendations and opinions can have indirect legal effect where they are preliminary to mandatory instruments subsequently passed or where the issuing institution has committed itself, thus generating legitimate expectations that must be satisfied.

The Community's international agreements

A third source of Community law has to do with its role at international level. As one of the focal points of the world, Europe cannot confine itself to managing its own internal affairs: it has to concern itself with economic, social and political relations with the world outside. The Community therefore concludes agreements in international law, with non-member countries and with other international organizations; these range from treaties providing for extensive cooperation in trade or in the industrial, technical and social fields to agreements on trade in particular products. With the Community's economic significance growing, and its trading activities expanding, the number of agreements it has concluded with non-member countries has increased substantially in the last few years.

Three kinds of agreement between the Community and non-member countries are particularly worth mentioning.

Association agreements (Article 238 EC)

Association is a special kind of relationship between the Community and a non-member country that goes beyond the mere regulation of trade and involves close economic cooperation and financial assistance. A distinction may be drawn between two different types of association agreement:

(i) Agreements that maintain special links between certain Member States and non-member countries.

One particular reason for the creation of the association agreement was the existence of overseas countries and territories with which Belgium, France, Italy and the Netherlands maintained particularly close ties as a legacy of their colonial empires. The introduction of a common external tariff in the Community would have seriously disrupted trade with these countries, so special arrangements needed to be made so that the system of unrestricted Community trade could be extended to them. At the same time tariffs on goods originating in these countries were progressively dismantled. Financial and technical assistance from the Community was channelled through the European Development Fund.

(ii) Agreements as preparation for accession to the Community or for the establishment of a customs union.

Association also has a role to play in the preparation of countries for possible membership of the Community. It serves as a preliminary stage towards accession during which the applicant country can work on converging its economy with that of the Community. This proved successful in the case of Greece, which was associated with the Community from 1962. Another association agreement with a view to future accession to the Community was concluded with Turkey in 1964.

Two other association agreements, whose eventual purpose is not membership of the Community but the establishment of a customs union, were concluded with Malta in 1971 and Cyprus in 1973. The EC has followed the same strategy in its relations with Central and Eastern Europe. Its 'Europe Agreements' with Poland, Hungary, the Czech Republic, Slovakia, Bulgaria and Romania make clear that Community membership is the ultimate goal for these countries in a process of far-reaching reform. The purpose of the association with them is to help them meet the conditions required for membership within the foreseeable future.

Cooperation agreements

Cooperation agreements are not as far-reaching as association agreements, being aimed solely at intensive economic cooperation. The Community has such agreements with the Maghreb States (Algeria, Morocco and Tunisia), the Mashreq States (Egypt, Jordan, Lebanon and Syria), and Israel, for instance.

The European Economic Area

The idea of establishing a European Economic Area bringing together the EC Member States and the members of the European Free Trade Area (Austria, Finland, Iceland, Liechtenstein, Norway, Sweden and Switzerland) was first mooted by the Commission President, Jacques Delors, in an address to the European Parliament on 17 January 1989, when he called for relations between the EC and EFTA to be reorganized in an association to develop into a co-decision system. What he said was this:

'There are two options open to us: we can stick to our present relations, essentially bilateral, with the ultimate aim of creating a free trade area encompassing the Community and EFTA, or, alternatively, we can look for a new, more structured partnership with common decision-making and administrative institutions to make our activities more effective...'.

The EFTA States responded favourably, and after lengthy negotiations the Agreement on the European Economic Area was signed on 2 May 1992. In the EEA, on the basis of the *acquis communautaire* (the body of primary and secondary legislation), there is to be free movement of goods, persons, services and capital, uniform rules on competition and State aid, and closer cooperation on horizontal and flanking policies (environment, R&D, education). The EEA thus brings the EFTA States into the internal market and, by requiring them to incorporate nearly two thirds of the EC's legislation, lays a firm basis for subsequent accession.

The Agreement's entry into force was delayed by the vote against it in the Swiss referendum, which also created the need for negotiations to adjust it to a new situation. These being now completed, the Agreement can come into force without Switzerland.

General principles of law

The sources of Community law described so far share a common feature in that they all produce written law. Like all systems of law, however, the Community legal order cannot consist entirely of written rules: there will always be gaps which have to be filled by unwritten law. The sources of unwritten Community law are provided by the general principles of law. These are rules reflecting the elementary concepts of law and justice that must be respected by any system of law. Written Community law for the most part deals only with economic and social matters, and is only to a limited extent capable of laying down rules of this kind, so that the general principles of law form one of the most important sources of law in the Community. They allow gaps to be filled and questions of the interpretation of existing law to be settled in the fairest way. These principles are given effect when the law is applied, particularly in the judgments of the Court of Justice: under Article 164 EEC, Article 136 Euratom and Article 31 ECSC 'the Court of Justice shall ensure that in the interpretation and application of this Treaty the law is observed'. The main points of reference for determining the general principles of law are the principles common to the legal orders of the Member States. They provide the background against which the rule needed to resolve a problem at Community level can be developed. So far the following principles have been formulated by the Court in this way, and thus recognized as sources of law in the Community legal order:

(i) aspects of the Community's liability for damage sustained as a result of action by its institutions or staff;

(ii) the principle of proportionality, whereby Community action must be relevant and necessary to the attainment of a Community objective and the aggregate burdens borne by all those affected must be no greater than what is needed for the attainment of that objective;

(iii) the principle that legitimate expectations must be protected: the Community's citizens and firms organize their lives on the basis of Community law and subsequent changes must therefore not be retroactive unless there is a serious Community interest to justify it and proper regard is had to legitimate expectations aroused;

(iv) the *ne bis in idem* principle (rule against double jeopardy), whereby any decision by a Community institution imposing a penalty must take into account earlier decisions taken by national authorities imposing penalties;

(v) fundamental human rights.

Agreements between the Member States

The final source of Community law is provided by agreements between the Member States. Agreements of this kind may be concluded when questions have to be settled that are closely linked to the Community's activities, but no powers have been transferred to the Community institutions; there are also full-scale international agreements (treaties and conventions) between the Member States aimed especially at overcoming the drawbacks of territorially limited arrangements and creating law that applies uniformly throughout the Community (see Article 220 EC) This is important primarily in the field of private international law; thus agreements have been concluded on the reciprocal recognition and enforcement of judgments in civil and commercial matters (1968) and on the mutual recognition of companies and legal persons (1968).

■ THE LEGISLATIVE PROCESS IN THE COMMUNITY

The legislative process is another area where the specific characteristics distinguishing the Community from a State are visible. Whereas in a State the will of the people will usually be expressed in parliament, the Council of the Community expresses the will of the governments of the Member States, simply because the Community does not consist of a European nation but owes its existence and form to the combined input of its several Member States. They did not transfer their sovereignty in part to the EC without further ado but pooled it on the understanding that they would retain the joint power to exercise it. But as the process of Community integration has developed and deepened, this division of powers in the Community decision-making process, originally oriented towards the defence of national interests by the Member States, has evolved into something much more balanced with regular enhancements of the status of the European Parliament.

The EC legislative process operates on three main levels, with different procedures applying at each of them. For instruments of general validity (regulations and directives) there is the proposal procedure, the cooperation procedure introduced by the Single European Act and the co-decision procedure introduced by the Treaty on European Union. Implementing measures are adopted by specific procedures. There is a simplified procedure for binding individual decisions and non-mandatory instruments. And ECSC instruments are in some cases subject to their own specific procedures.

The proposal procedure

The proposal procedure is, as it always was, the basis for the adoption of all general EC instruments; it is applicable where neither the cooperation procedure nor the co-decision procedure is stated to apply. It rests on a division of labour between the Council and the Commission. Put very briefly, the Commission proposes and the Council disposes. But before the Council actually reaches a decision there are various stages to be completed in which, depending on the subject of the measure, it may also come before the European Parliament and the Economic and Social Committee.

The formulation stage

The machinery is set in motion by the Commission, which draws up a proposal for the measure in question (we therefore speak of the Commission's right of initiative). A proposal is prepared on the responsibility of a Member of the Commission by the Commission department dealing with the particular field; frequently the department will also consult national experts at this stage. The draft drawn up here, which is a complete text, setting out the content and form of the measure to the last detail, goes before the Commission as a whole, when a simple majority is enough to have it adopted. It is now a 'Commission proposal', and is sent to the Council with a detailed explanation of the grounds for it.

The consultation stage

The Council first checks whether it must consult other Community bodies before deciding on the proposal. The treaties give the European Parliament the right to be consulted on all politically important measures ('compulsory consultation'). Parliament here speaks on behalf of all the citizens of the Community; its function is to look after their interest in the development of the Community. Failure to consult Parliament in such cases is a serious irregularity and an infringement of the treaties. Apart from compulsory consultation of this kind, Parliament is in practice also consulted on all other draft legislation (optional consultation). Parliament's part in the process ends with the adoption of a formal written opinion, which the President of Parliament transmits to the Council and the Commission, and which may recommend amendments to the proposal. But the Council is not legally obliged to take account of the opinions or amendments emanating from Parliament.

As well as the European Parliament the treaties in some cases also oblige the Council to consult the Economic and Social Committee. Consultation of the Committee is explicitly required, for example, for Council measures relating to the freedom of establishment (see Article 54(2) EC). But the Council is free to consult the Committee in other cases too. This is done very frequently, although it is not the general rule as it is with Parliament. As in the case of Parliament, the Economic and Social Committee's opinion on the proposal is sent to the Council and the Commission, and this ends its part in the process. But the Committee's opinion, like that of Parliament, is not binding on the Council.

The enactment stage

After Parliament and the Economic and Social Committee have been consulted, the Commission proposal is once more put before the Council, perhaps amended by the Commission in the light of the opinions of Parliament and the Committee (see Article 189a EC).* It will first be discussed by specialized working parties and then by the Permanent Representatives Committee. The importance of this Committee in the workings of the Community can hardly be exaggerated. It is in permanent session, and coordinates the preparatory work for Council meetings, determining the priorities and urgency of the items on the Ministers' agenda when they meet in the Council. It can also reach agreement on technical points, with the Ministers merely rubber-stamping measures adopted unanimously by the Permanent Representatives. Adoption of the proposal by the Council is the final stage in the legislative process.

Publication: The final text, in all nine official languages of the Community (Danish, Dutch, English, French, German, Greek, Italian, Portuguese and Spanish), is adopted by the Council, signed by the President of the Council, and published in the *Official Journal of the European Communities* or notified to the person to whom it is addressed (Article 191 EC).

The cooperation procedure (Article 189c EC)*

The cooperation procedure is substantially inspired by the proposal procedure described above but involves a much stronger role for Parliament and operates much more quickly. It is applicable primarily in matters relating to the internal market, social policy, economic and social cohesion and R&D. Decisions may be taken by qualified majority unless they concern taxation, the free movement of workers and their rights and interests, in which case the unanimity rule applies.

---

* Formerly Article 149(1) EEC.

* Formerly Article 149(2) EEC.

The cooperation procedure is briefly as follows:

1. As in the proposal procedure, the procedure begins with a Commission proposal. But it is not sent just to the Council: il also goes to Parliament, which after a first reading notifies the Council of its opinion.

2. On the basis of the Commission's proposal, Parliament's opinion and its own deliberations, the Council adopts a common position, which is sent to Parliament for its second reading. Parliament now has three months to do one of four things:

(i) It may accept the Council's common position, in which case the Council may adopt the instrument.

(ii) It may refrain from reacting, in which case it is deemed to have accepted the Council's common position and the Council may adopt it.

(iii) It may reject the common position, in which case unanimity is required for the adoption of the instrument by the Council.

Given the difficulty of achieving unanimity in the Council, the proposal is effectively lost. Only rarely will Parliament block legislation in this way.

(iv) It may, and usually does, propose amendments to the common position. The question is then whether the Commission accepts its amendments. If it does, the Council may adopt the instrument in the usual way, by a qualified majority or (if it is departing from the Commission's proposal) unanimously. If the Commission does not accept them, their adoption by the Council requires a unanimous vote.

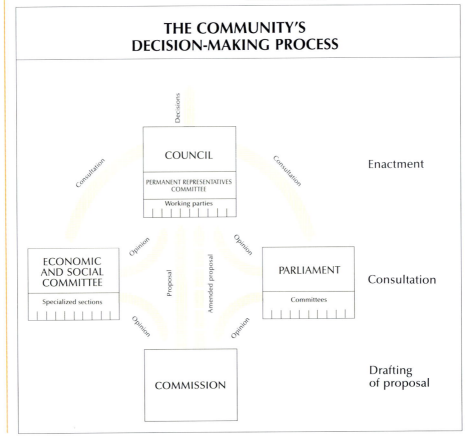

In any case, the Council may still exercise a veto by not taking any decision on the amendments proposed by Parliament or on the amended Commission proposal, thereby blocking the legislation in question. However, on the whole, the cooperation procedure is a considerable step forward in the Community's decision-making process.

The co-decision procedure (Article 189b EC)

The following is a simplified description of the co-decision procedure:

1. Here again, the starting point is a Commission proposal that is sent to the Council and Parliament. Parliament takes its first reading and sends its opinion to the Council.

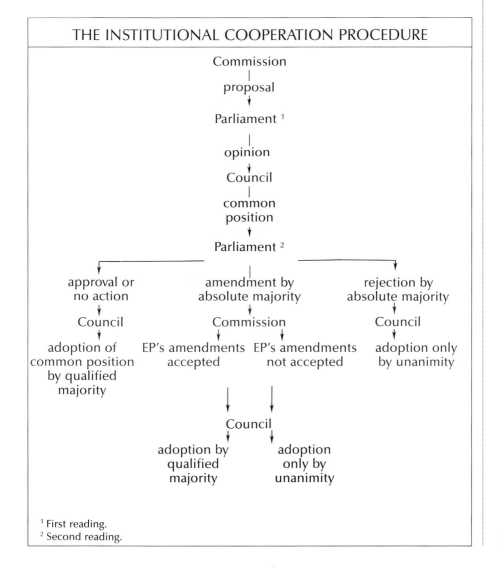

THE INSTITUTIONAL COOPERATION PROCEDURE

[1] First reading.
[2] Second reading.

2. On the basis of the Commission's proposal, Parliament's opinion and its own deliberations, the Council adopts a common position, by a qualified mojority if it accepts the Commission's proposal or unanimously if it wishes to depart from it. The common position is then sent to Parliament for its second reading. Parliament is now at the co-decision stage and has three months in which to do one of three things:

(i) It may accept the Council's common position or refrain from reacting to it, in which case the Council may adopt the instrument.

(ii) If it wishes, it may make amendments to the common position. The procedure is then that a Conciliation Committee of representatives of the Council and Parliament (in equal proportions) is set up to negotiate a compromise. If a compromise is agreed on, the instrument is adopted accordingly by joint decision of the Council and Parliament.

(iii) It may reject the common position outright, in which case the Council may convene the Conciliation Committee and the procedure is then as above.

3. Where the Conciliation Committee fails to agree on a compromise draft, the Council may within six weeks confirm its common position, amended as desired by Parliament, by a qualified majority, but Pariament may still reject it by an absolute majority of its members at third reading. In this event the proposal is lost; Parliament has an effective right of veto.

The introduction of the co-decision procedure constitutes both a challenge and an opportunity for Parliament. If the procedure is to operate successfully, there must be an agreement in the Conciliation Committee, but there are the beginnings of a radically new relationship between Parliament and the Council. For the first time the two institutions are placed on an equal footing in the legislative process. It will now be up to Parliament to demonstrate its capacity for compromise and to direct its energies in the Conciliation Committee towards coming to an agreement with the Council. In practice the co-decision procedure is by no means confined to areas of lesser political interest, for it encompasses the free movement of workers, freedom of establishment (including special rules for foreign nationals and recognition of diplomas), freedom to provide services, the harmonization of legislation for the establishment and operation of the single market, education and vocational training, youth, culture and health, consumer protection, R&D and certain environmental programmes.

The procedure for implementing measures

The general rule is that the Council confers on the Commission the power to issue measures implementing its instrument (Article 145 EC). Only in special cases may the Council reserve implementing powers for itself. When exercising its implementing powers the Commission may neither amend nor supplement the Council instrument; if that is necessary, one of three committee procedures will be applied, as specified in the enabling instrument.

The Advisory Committee procedure: This procedure applies chiefly to measures required for the implementation of Council instruments for the achievement of the single market. The Advisory Committee is made up of representatives of the Member States and chaired by a Commission representative. The Commission representative present a draft of the measures to be taken, and the Committee gives its opinion on them within a time limit set by the Commission. The Commission is expected, though not obliged, to take the fullest possible account of the opinion; it informs the Committee of the action taken on its suggestions and proposed amendments.

The Management Committee procedure: This procedure has been applied for agricultural regulations since 1962. Before adopting implementing measures, the Com-

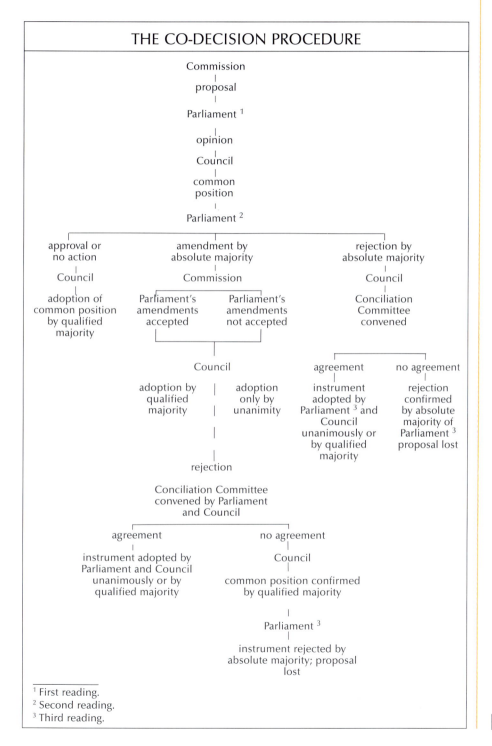

mission first consults a Management Committee composed of representatives of the Member States, which gives an opinion on them by qualified majority (Article 148(2) EC). If the Committee approves the measures, the Commission may put them into effect. Otherwise, the Commission may forthwith adopt measures and immediately notify the Council of them. The Council may then, within one month (variant a) or three months (variant b), take a different decision.

The Legislation Committee procedure: This procedure, established by the Council in 1968, applies to other areas of Community activity. The Committee likewise consists of representatives of the Member States and gives its opinion on the Commission's proposed implementing measures by qualified majority. The difference between this procedure and the Management Committee procedure lies in the Commission's much weaker position where the Committee rejects the proposed measures or fails to give an opinion. The Commission cannot put its measures immediately into effect but must propose them for a Council decision. The Council must take its decision on this proposal by qualified majority within three months. If it does not do so, the Commission may then put its measures into effect (variant a), unless the Council adopts a different decision by qualified majority (variant b).

The simplified procedure

The simplified procedure, where no Commission proposal is needed to initiate the legislative process, applies to measures within the Commission's own powers and also to non-mandatory instruments (recommendations and opinions) issued by the Commission or the Council.

Specific ECSC procedures

The procedure is different in the case of the binding legal instruments of the ECSC, the general decision and the ECSC recommendation. The main difference from the scheme laid down in the Rome Treaties lies in the role of the Commission and the Council. The ECSC Treaty gives the power to adopt these instruments not to the Council but, generally, to the Commission. In certain specified cases they require the Council's assent, and of course this does then enable the Council to block Commission measures. Before the Commission finally adopts a text it must, in certain cases laid down by the Treaty, consult Parliament and the ECSC Consultative Committee.

■ LEGALITY OF THE ACTS OF THE COMMUNITY INSTITUTIONS

The Community treaties attach great importance to the principle that the acts of the institutions must be in accordance with the provisions of the treaties. This principle is expressed in many of their provisions: for example, all three treaties, in connection with the tasks of the Community and its institutions, use the expressions 'in accordance with the provisions of this Treaty', 'as provided in this Treaty' and 'pursuant to this Treaty'. Just as the Community institutions are bound by the law laid down in the treaties when exercising their legislative and executive authority, so they must observe Community secondary law when enacting implementing provisions and dealing with particular cases by means of individual decisions. The comprehensive rules of Community law, sometimes quite specific even on points of detail, would have little point if the Community institutions were not bound to observe them scrupulously.

■ COMMUNITY SYSTEM OF LEGAL PROTECTION

Like every legal order, the Community legal order provides a self-contained system of legal protection to deal with disputes concerning Community law and to ensure its implementation. The focal point of this system is the Court of Justice of the European Communities and the associated Court of First Instance. It is the supreme and, at the same time, the only judicial authority empowered to determine all questions of Community law. Its general task is described in the founding treaties as being to 'ensure that in the interpretation and application of this Treaty the law is observed'. (Article 164 EC, Article 136 Euratom, Article 31 ECSC). The Court's duties are extremely wide-ranging. First, it acts in an advisory capacity: it can deliver opinions on conventions the Community intends to conclude with States or international organizations. These opinions are legally binding. Of much greater importance, however, are its functions as a judicial body. They embrace the following types of proceedings:

Treaty infringement proceedings (Article 169 EC)

There is a procedure for establishing whether a Member State has failed to fulfil an obligation imposed on it by Community law. Given the seriousness of the accusation, the referral of the Court of Justice must be preceded by a preliminary procedure in which the Member State is given the opportunity to present its observations. If the dispute is not settled at that stage, either the Commission or another Member State may commence an action in the Court. In practice the initiative is usually taken by the Commission. The Court investigates the complaint and decided whether the Treaty is infringed. If so, the offending Member State is then required to take the measures needed to conform. If a Member State fails to comply with a judgment given against it, the Treaty on European Union offers a new possibility of ordering it to pay a lump-sum fine or a penalty payment (Article 171 EC, as amended at Maastricht).

Actions for annulment (Article 173 EC)

These actions are to have Council or Commission instruments annulled. They may be based on allegations of *ultra vires,* violation of essential procedural requirements, infringement of the Treaties or secondary legislation, or abuse of discretion. They may be brought by a Member State, the Council or the Commission. The Court of Justice has held that they may be brought by Parliament where it can show that the enacting institution has violated the rights conferred on it by the Community treaties. But citizens and firms can only proceed against decisions that are personally addressed to them or, though addressed to others, have a direct individual effect on them. If the action succeeds, the Court may declare the instrument void with retroactive effect; in certain circumstances, it may declare it void solely from the date of the judgment. By the Council Decision of 8 June 1993, actions for annulment brought by citizens and firms will lie in the Court of First Instance, except where they relate to anti-dumping matters.

Complaints for failure to act (Article 175 EC Treaty)

This form of action supplements the legal protection available against the Council and the Commission; it lies where the institution has unlawfully failed to take a decision. There is a preliminary procedure whereby the complainant must first put the institution on notice to perform its duty. The order sought in an action by the Council, the Commission or Parliament is a declaration that the Council or the Commission has infringed the Treaty by neglecting to take a decision required of it. Where the action is brought by a citizen or a firm, it is for a declaration that the institution has infringed the Treaty by neglecting to address an individual decision to them. The judgment simply finds that the neglect was unlawful. The Court of Justice has no jurisdiction to order that a decision be taken: the party against whom judgment is given is merely required in the usual way to take measures to comply with the judgment.

Actions for damages
(Article 178 and the second paragraph of Article 215 EC)

Citizens and firms that sustain damage by reason of fault committed by EC staff have the possibility to proceed for damages in the Court of Justice. The basis for Community liability is set rather laconically by the treaties; for the rest, it is governed by the general principles common to the laws of the Member States. The Court has fleshed this out, holding that the following conditions must be satisfied before an award of damages can be made:

(i) There must be an unlawful act by a Community institution or by a member of its staff in the exercise of his functions as such.

Where the case turns on liability for a legislative instrument (regulation or directive) unlawfully made by the institution, it is not enough that the instrument be unlawful: it must be in substantial and manifest conflict with a superior rule of law having the purpose of protecting individual rights. It is no easy matter to determine when there is a serious enough violation of Community law. The Court tends to have regard to the narrowness of the category of persons affected by the offending measure and the scale of the damage sustained, which must be in excess of the commercial risk that it is reasonable to expect the relevant branch of economic life to accept.

(ii) There must be actual damage.

(iii) There must be a causal link between the act of the Community institution and the damage sustained.

(iv) Intent or negligence do not have to be proved. Actions for damages are within the jurisdiction of the Court of First Instance.

Staff disputes (Article 179 EC)

The Court of First Instance also has jurisdiction in disputes arising between staff members or their surviving family members and their employing institution from the employment relationship.

Preliminary rulings (Article 177 EC)

This is the procedure whereby the national courts can seek guidance on Community law from the Court of Justice. Where a national court is required to apply provisions of Community law in a case before it, it may stay the proceedings and ask the Court of Justice questions regarding the validity of the Community instrument at issue and/or the interpretation of the instrument and of the treaties. The Court of Justice answers the question in a judgment, not in an advisory opinion; this highlights the mandatory nature of its ruling. The preliminary ruling procedure, unlike the other procedures considered here, is not a contentious procedure but simple one stage in the proceedings that begins and ends in the national court. The object is to secure a uniform interpretation of Community law and, with it, the unity of the Community legal order.

The broad lines of the preliminary ruling procedure can be summed up as follows:

1. Subject-matter. The Court of Justice rules on the validity and interpretation of instruments of Community law but not of national instruments.

2. Capacity to proceed. The procedure is available to all independent official dispute-settlement authorities, 'independent' meaning not bound by instructions. The national court's decision whether or not to make a reference will depend on the importance of the point of Community law in issue for the settlement of the dispute before it, which is a matter for the national court to assess. The parties can only request, not require it to make a reference. The Court of Justice considers the importance of the point solely in terms of whether there is indeed a point of law to be examined that has not already been settled.

3. Obligation to refer. A national court or tribunal against whose decision there is no judicial remedy in national law is obliged to refer, unless the question is of no material importance for the outcome of the case before it or has already been answered by the Court of Justice or the interpretation of Community law is not open to reasonable doubt. But the obligation to refer is unconditional where the validity of a Community instrument is in issue. Failure to discharge the obligation to refer can be penalized in both national and Community law. In Community terms it would constitute an infringement of the EC Treaty, of Article 177 to be precise, exposing the relevant Member State to infringement proceedings under Article 169. But so far this has never been necessary. In national terms there will be the question of the validity of a judgment given in disregard of obligations flowing from Community law.

4. Effect. The preliminary ruling is directly binding on the referring court and all other courts hearing the same case. And in practice it has a very high status as a precedent for subsequent cases of like nature.

THE POSITION OF COMMUNITY LAW IN RELATION TO THE LEGAL ORDER AS A WHOLE

After all that we have learnt about the structure of the Community and its legal order, it is not easy to assign Community law its rightful place in the legal order as a whole and to define the boundaries between it and other legal orders. Two possible approaches to classifying it must be rejected from the outset. Community law must not be conceived of as a mere collection of international agreements, nor can it be viewed as a part or an appendage of national legal systems.

■ THE AUTONOMY OF THE COMMUNITY LEGAL ORDER

On the contrary, through the establishment of the Community, the Member States have limited their legislative sovereignty and in so doing have created a self-sufficient body of law that is binding on them and on their nationals.

One of the best-known cases heard in the Court of Justice was *Costa v ENEL* in 1964. In 1962 Italy had nationalized electricity generation and distribution and vested the business of the former electricity companies in ENEL, the new public corporation. Mr Costa lost his rights to dividends formerly payable to him as a shareholder in Edison Volta as a result of the nationalization and declined to pay an electricity bill for LIT 1 926 by way of self-compensation. In the Milan court his argument was that the nationalization act was contrary to a range of provisions of the EEC Treaty. The court referred questions on the interpretation of these provisions to the Court of Justice. The Italian Government pleaded that the reference was 'absolutely inadmissible' since the national court could apply only national law and had no business presenting the case to the Court of Justice. The Court's answer was unequivocal:

'By contrast with ordinary international treaties, the EEC Treaty has created its own legal system which, on the entry into force of the Treaty, became an integral part of the legal systems of the Member States and which their courts are bound to apply.

By creating a Community of unlimited duration, having its own institutions, its own legal capacity ... and, more particularly, real powers ..., the Member States have limited their sovereign rights, albeit within limited fields, and have thus created a body of law which binds both their nationals and themselves.'

The autonomy of the Community legal order is of fundamental significance for the nature of the EC, for it is the only guarantee that Community law will not be watered down be the interaction with national law and that it will apply uniformly throughout the Community. This is why the concepts of Community law are interpreted in the light of the purposes pursued by Community law and the Community in general. This specific teleological interpretation technique is indispensable since specific rights are secured by Community law and without it they would be endangered, for each Member State could then, by interpreting provisions in different ways, decide individually on the substance of the freedoms that Community law is supposed to generate. As an example, consider the concept of the worker, on which the scope of the concept of freedom of movement is based. The specific Community concept of the worker is quite capable of deviating from the concepts that are known and applied in the legal orders of the Member States.

Against the backdrop of this concept of the autonomy of the Community legal order, what is the relationship between Community law and national law?

Even if Community law constitutes a legal order that is self-sufficient in relation to the legal orders of the Member States, this situation must not be regarded as one in which the Community legal order and the legal orders of the Member States are superimposed on one another like layers of bedrock. The fact that they are applicable to the same people, who thus become citizens of a national State and citizens of the Community in one person, negates such a rigid demarcation of these legal orders. Secondly, such an approach disregards the fact that Community law can become operational only if it becomes part of the legal orders of the Member States. The truth is that the Community legal order and the national legal orders are interlocked and mutually dependent on one another.

■ COOPERATION BETWEEN COMMUNITY LAW AND NATIONAL LAW

This aspect of the interaction between Community law and national law covers those areas where the two systems supplement each other. Article 5 of the EC Treaty is clear enough:

'Member States shall take all appropriate measures, whether general or particular, to ensure fulfilment of the obligations arising out of this Treaty or resulting from action taken by the institutions of the Community. They shall facilitate the achievement of the Community's tasks.

They shall abstain from any measure which could jeopardize the attainment of the objectives of this Treaty.'

This general principle was inspired by an awareness that the Community legal order on its own is not able to fully achieve the objectives pursued by the establishment of the EC. Unlike a national legal order, the Community legal order is not a self-contained system but relies on the support of the national systems for its operation. All three branches of government — the legislative, the executive and the judicial — therefore need to acknowledge that the Community legal order is not a 'foreign' system but that the Member States and the Community institutions have established indissoluble links between themselves so as to achieve their common objectives. The EC is not just a community of interests; it is a community of solidarity. It follows that national authorities are required not only to observe the Community treaties and secondary legislation; they must also implement them and bring them to life. The interaction between the two systems is so thoroughly multifaceted that a few examples are called for.

The first illustration of the way in which the Community and national legal orders mesh with each other and complement each other is the directive, already considered in the chapter on legislation. All the directive itself fixes in binding terms is the result to be achieved by the Member State; it is for national authorities, via domestic law, to decide how and by what means the result is then actually achieved. In the judicial area, the two systems mesh through the preliminary ruling procedure of Article 177 of the EC Treaty, whereby national courts may, or sometimes must, refer questions on the interpretation and validity of Community law to the Court of Justice, whose ruling may well be of decisive authority in the settlement of the dispute before them. Two things are clear. For one, the court in the Member States are required to observe and apply Community law; for another, the interpretation of Community law and declarations as to its validity are the sole preserve of the Court of Justice. The interdependence of Community and national law is further illustrated by what happens when gaps in Community law need to be filled in, as where Community law makes a *renvoi* to existing rules of national law to complete the rules it itself determines. The fate of the relevant rules of Community law will then largely depend on the national rules. An example of this is to be found in Article 192 of the EC Treaty, which reads:

'Decisions of the Council or the Commission which impose a pecuniary obligation on persons other than States shall be enforceable.

Enforcement shall be governed by the rules of civil procedure in force in the State in the territory of which it is carried out...'

This principle is actually applicable to the full range of obligations under Community law has not itself determined rules for its enforcement. In any such case, national authorities enforce Community law by means of the substantive and procedural provisions of their own legal systems. But the principle is subject to one proviso: the uniformity of the application of Community law must be preserved, for it would be wholly unacceptable for citizens and firms to be affected unequally — and therefore unjustly — by it.

■ CONFLICT BETWEEN COMMUNITY LAW AND NATIONAL LAW

However, the relationship between Community law and national law is also characterized by an occasional 'hostility' between the Community legal order and the national legal orders. Here one speaks of a conflict between Community law and national law. Such a situation always arises when a provision of Community law confers rights and imposes obligations directly upon Community citizens while its content conflicts with a rule of national law. Concealed behind this apparently simple problem area are two fundamental questions underlying the construction of the Community, the answers to which were destined to become the acid test for the existence of the Community legal order, namely:

(i) the direct applicability of Community law and

(ii) the primacy of Community law over conflicting national law.

Direct applicability of Community law

Firstly, the direct applicability of Community law simply means that the latter confers rights and imposes obligations directly not only on the Community institutions and the Member States but also on the Community's citizens. That bald statement does not, however, get us very far since the question remains which provisions of Community law have that effect. The Community treaties enlighten us in this regard only by reference to what is referred to as secondary legislation (enacted by the institutions). For example, Article 189(2) EC states that a regulation is 'directly applicable in all Member States'.

One of the outstanding achievements of the Court of Justice of the European Communities is that is has enforced the direct applicability of the provisions of Community law despite the initial resistance of certain Member States and has thus guaranteed the existence of the Community legal order. Its case-law on this point started with a perfectly run-of-the-mill case which, however, was destined to go down in the annals of the Court. In this case, a Dutch transport firm, Van Gend & Loos, brought an action in a Dutch court against the Dutch customs authorities, who had charged increased customs duties on a chemical product imported from the Federal Republic of Germany. The firm regarded this practice as an infringement of Article 12 EEC, which prohibited the Member States from introducing new customs duties or increasing those that they already applied in the common market. In the final analysis, the outcome of these proceedings depended on the question whether individuals, also, can rely on Article 12 against customs duties levied in breach of the Treaty. As the answer to this question necessitated an interpretation of the EEC Treaty, the Dutch court suspended the proceedings and referred the matter to the Court of Justice. Despite the advice of numerous governments and its Advocate-General, the Court decided that all the rules of the founding treaties, which are worded uncondi-

tionally, are self-sufficient and legally complete so that their implementation or validity does not require any further intervention by the Member States or the Commission, can apply directly to individuals. This was stated to be the case with Article 12, so that the Van Gend & Loos company could also derive rights from that provision which the Dutch court had to protect. The logical consequence was that the customs duties levied in breach of the Treaty were declared void. In the grounds for its judgment, the Court stated that 'the Community constitutes a new legal order... the subjects of which comprise not only the Member States but also their nationals. Independently of the legislation of Member States, Community law not only imposes obligations on individuals but is also intended to confer upon them rights. These rights arise not only where they are expressly granted by the Treaty, but also by reason of obligations which the Treaty imposes in a clearly defined way upon individuals as well as upon the Member States and upon the institutions of the Community'.

Subsequently, the Court continued to apply this reasoning in regard to provisions of the EEC Treaty that are of far greater importance to citizens of the Community than Article 12. Three judgments are noteworthy here covering the direct application of Article 48 (freedom of movement), Article 52 (freedom of establishment) and Article 59 (freedom to provide services).

With regard to the guarantees afforded by Article 48, the Court of Justice delivered a judgment declaring the article directly applicable in the *Van Duyn* case. The facts of this case were as follows: a Miss van Duyn, a Dutch national, was, in May 1973, refused leave to enter the United Kingdom in order to take up employment as a secretary with the 'Church of Scientology', an organization considered by the Home Office to be 'socially harmful'. Relying on the Community rules on freedom of movement for workers, in particular Article 48 EEC, Miss van Duyn brought an action before the High Court. She sought a declaration from the High Court that she was entitled to stay in the United Kingdom for the purpose of employment and to be given leave to enter the United Kingdom. In answer to a question referred by the High Court, the Court of Justice held that Article 48 has direct effect and hence confers on individuals rights that are enforceable before the courts of a Member State.

The Court of Justice was asked by the Belgian Conseil d'Etat to give a ruling on the direct effect of Article 52. The Conseil d'Etat had to decide an action brought by a Dutch lawyer, J. Reyners, who wished to assert his rights arising out of Article 52. Mr Reyners felt obliged to bring the action after he had been denied admission to the profession of lawyer in Belgium because of his foreign nationality, despite the fact that he had passed the necessary Belgian examinations. In its judgment of 21 July 1974, the Court held that unequal treatment of nationals and foreigners as regards establishment could no longer be maintained, as Article 52 was directly applicable since the end of the transitional period and hence entitled Community citizens to take up and pursue gainful employment in another Member State in the same way as a national. As a result of this judgment Mr Reyners had to be admitted to the legal profession in Belgium.

The Court of Justice was given an opportunity in the *Van Binsbergen* case to establish expressly the direct effect of Article 59 EEC. These proceedings involved *inter alia* the question whether a Dutch legal provision to the effect that only persons habitually resident in the Netherlands could act as legal representatives before an appeal court is compatible with the Community rules on freedom to provide services. The Court answered this question in the negative on the ground that all restrictions to which Community citizens might be subject by reason of their nationality or place of residence infringe Article 59 and are therefore void.

Of the many other treaty provisions whose direct effect within a Member State the Court has confirmed, the following may be singled out: Article 30 EC, which guarantees freedom of movement for goods, and Article 119 EC, which guarantees equal pay for men and women.

Since 1970 the Court has extended its principles concerning direct effect to provisions in directives and in decisions addressed to States. This seems logical if even treaty law can apply directly to Community citizens despite the fact that it is addressed first and foremost to the Member States.

The practical importance of the direct effect of Community law in the form in which it has been developed and brought to fruition by the Court of Justice can scarcely be overemphasized. It improves the position of the individual by turning the freedoms of the common market into rights that may be enforced in a national court of law. The direct effect of Community law is therefore one of the pillars, as it were, of the Community legal order.

Primacy of Community law

The direct effect of a provision of Community law leads to a second, equally fundamental question: what happens if a provision of Community law gives rise to direct rights and obligations for the Community citizen and conflicts in substance with a rule of national law?

Such a conflict between Community law and national law can be settled only if one gives way to the other. Community legislation contains no express provision on the question. None of the Community treaties contains a provision stating, for example, that Community law overrides national law or that it is inferior to national law. Nevertheless, the only way of settling conflicts between Community law and national law is to grant Community law primacy over national law and allow it to supersede all national provisions that diverge from a Community rule and take their place in the national legal orders. After all, what would remain of the Community legal order if Community law were to be subordinated to national law? Hardly anything! Community rules could be set aside by any national law. There would no longer be any question of a uniform and equal application of Community law in all Member States. Nor would the Community be able to perform the tasks entrusted to it by the Member States. The ability of the Community to function would be jeopardized, and the construction of a united Europe on which so many hopes rest would never be achieved.

Once again it fell to the Court of Justice of the Community, in view of these consequences, to establish — despite opposition from several Member States — the principle of the primacy of Community law that is essential to the existence of the Community legal order. In so doing, it erected the second pillar of the Community legal order after direct effect, which was to turn that legal order at last into a sound edifice. In *Costa v ENEL*, the Court made two important observations regarding the relationship between Community law and national law:

Firstly: the Member States have definitively transferred sovereign rights to a Community created by them. They cannot reverse this process by means of subsequent unilateral measures inconsistent with the Community concept.

Secondly: it is a principle of the Treaty that no Member State may call into question the status of Community law as a system uniformly and generally applicable throughout the Community.

It follows from this that Community law, which was enacted in accordance with the powers laid down in the Treaties, has priority over any conflicting law of the Member States. Not only is it stronger than earlier national law, but it also has a limiting effect on laws adopted subsequently.

Ultimately, the Court did not in its judgment call in question the nationalization of the Italian electricity industry, but it quite emphatically established the primacy of Community law over national law.

The Court has since adhered to this finding in case after case. It has, in fact, developed it further in one respect. Whereas in the judgment just mentioned it was concerned only with the question of the primacy of Community law over ordinary national laws, it confirmed the principle of primacy with regard also to the relationship between Community law and national constitutional law. After initial hesitation, national courts in principle accepted the interpretation of the Court of Justice. In the Netherlands no difficulties could arise in any case as the primacy of treaty law over national statute law is expressly laid down in the constitution (Articles 65 to 67). In the other Member States the principle of the primacy of Community law over national law has likewise been recognized by national courts. However, the constitutional courts of Germany and Italy initially refused to accept the primacy of Community law over national constitutional law, in particular regarding the guaranteed protection of fundamental rights. They abandoned their objections only after the protection of fundamental rights in the Community legal order had reached a standard that corresponded in essence to that of their national constitutions. Since then the primacy of Community law even over national constitutional law has been generally recognized.

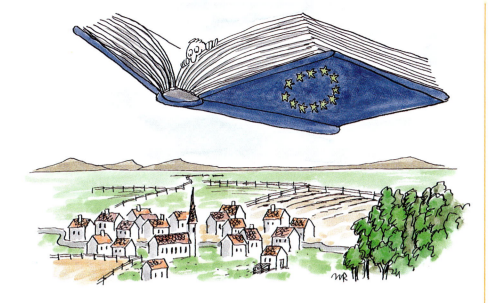

CONCLUSIONS

What overall picture emerges of the construction of the European Community and its legal order?

The European Communities have a relatively uniform system of rules — their constitution. Crucial factors in its creation were the comparable state of economic development of the original Member States and their broad consensus on the means and objectives of the unification of Europe. The similarity of Member States' values and the existence of a model were decisive when it came to choosing a constitutional system.

The legal order is the true foundation of the Community, giving it a common system of law on which to operate. Only by creating new law and upholding it can the objectives pursued by setting up the Community be achieved. The Community legal order has already accomplished a great deal in this respect. It is thanks not least to this new legal order that the, by and large, open frontiers, the substantial trade in goods and services, the migration of workers and the large number of transnational links between companies have already made the common market part of everyday life for approximately 360 million people. Another feature of the Community legal order that has already attained historic importance is its peacemaking role. With its objective of maintaining peace and liberty, it replaces force as a means of settling conflicts by rules of law that bind both individuals and the Member States into a single Community. As a result the Community legal order is an important instrument for the preservation and creation of peace.

The Community legal order and the Community that is based on it can survive only if observance and protection of the legal order are guaranteed. This is ensured by the two cornerstones of the Community legal order: the direct effect of Community law and the primacy of Community law over national law. These two principles, the existence and maintenance of which are defended with great determination by the Court of Justice, guarantee the uniform and priority application of Community law in all Member States.

For all its imperfections, the contribution the Community legal order makes towards solving the political, economic and social problems of the Member States of the Community is of inestimable value.

TABLE OF CASES

■ NATURE AND PRIMACY OF COMMUNITY LAW

Case 26/62 *Van Gend & Loos* [1963] ECR 1 (Nature of Community law; rights and obligations of individuals).

Case 6/64 *Costa* v *ENEL* [1964] ECR 585 (Nature of Community law; direct applicability; primacy of Community law).

Case 14/68 *Walt Wilhelm and Others* [1969] ECR 1 (Nature of Community law; primacy of Community law).

Case 106/77 *Simmenthal* [1978] ECR 269 (Community law; direct applicability; primacy).

Case 826/79 *Mireco* [1980] ECR 2559 (Primacy of Community law).

Case 104/86 *Commission* v *Italy* [1988] ECR 1813 (Nature of Community law; direct applicability).

Case 170/88 *Ford España* [1989] ECR 2339 (Conflict between national and Community law; direct applicability; primacy of Community law).

Case C-213 *Factortame* [1990] ECR I-2466 (Direct applicability; primacy of Community law).

Joined Cases 6 and 9/90 *Francovich* and *Bonifaci* [1991] ECR I-5403 (Effect of Community law; liability of Member States for failure to discharge Community obligations; non-transposal of directives).

Joined Cases C-13 and 113/91 *Debus*, judgment given on 4.6.1992, not yet reported (Conflict between national and Community law; direct applicability; primacy of Community law).

■ POWERS OF THE COMMUNITY

Case 8/55 *Fédéchar* [1954-56] ECR 245 (Implied powers; official fixing of prices).

Case 22/70 *AETR* [1971] ECR 263 (Legal personality and treaty-making powers of the Community).

Joined Cases 3, 4 and 6/76 *Kramer* [1976] ECR 1279 (External relations; international commitments; authority of the Community).

Opinion 1/76 [1977] ECR 741 (External relations; international commitments; authority of the Community).

Opinion 1/78 [1979] ECR 2871 (Division of powers between the Community and the Member States).

Joined Cases C-51, 90 and 94/89 *United Kingdom and others* v *Council* [1991] ECR I-2786 (Subsidiarity, scope of principle).

Opinion 2/91 given on 19.3.1991 (Distribution of powers between the Community and the Member States).

■ EFFECTS OF LEGAL ACTS

Case 43/71 *Politi* [1971] ECR 1039 (Regulations; direct effects).

Case 34/73 *Variola* [1973] ECR 981 (Regulations; direct effects).

Case 65/75 *Tasca* [1976] ECR 291 (Regulations; direct effects).

Case 31/78 *Bussone* [1978] ECR 2429 (Regulations; direct effects).

Case 177/78 *Pigs and Bacon Commission* [1979] ECR 2161 (Regulations; direct effects).

Case 2/74 *Reyners* [1974] ECR 631 (Direct applicability; freedom of establishment).

Case 11/77 *Patrick* [1977] ECR 1199 (Direct applicability; right of establishment).

Case 33/74 *Van Binsbergen* [1974] ECR 1299 (Direct applicability; freedom to provide services).

Case 41/74 *Van Duyn* [1974] ECR 1337 (Direct applicability; freedom of movement).

Case 9/70 *Grad* [1970] ECR 825 (Decisions; direct applicability).

Case 20/70 *Transports Lesage & Cie* [1970] ECR 861 (Decisions; direct applicability).

Case 33/70 *SACE* [1970] ECR 1213 (Directives; direct applicability).

Case 148/78 *Ratti* [1979] ECR 1629 (Directives; direct applicability).

Case 70/83 *Kloppenburg* [1984] ECR 1075 (Directives; direct applicability).

Case 152/84 *Marshall* [1986] ECR 723 (Directives; direct applicability).

Case 31/87 *Beentjes* [1988] ECR 4635 (Directives; direct applicability).

Case 103/88 *Costanzo* [1989] ECR 1861 (Directives; direct effect; conditions precedent; consequences).

Case 322/88 *Grimaldi* [1989] ECR 4416 (Recommendations; direct effect or its absence; observance by national courts).

Case C-188/89 *Foster* [1990] ECR I-3343 (Directives; horizontal direct effect).

Case C-221, 88 *Busseni* [1990] ECR I-519 (ECSC recommendations/directives; vertical direct effect).

Case C-292/89 *Antonissen* [1991] ECR I-773 (Statements in Council minutes; status for interpretation purposes).

Case C-156/91 *Hansa Fleisch*, judgment given on 10.11.1992, not yet reported (Decisions; direct applicability; conditions precedent).

■ FUNDAMENTAL RIGHTS

Case 29/69 *Stauder* [1969] ECR 419 (Fundamental rights; general principles of law).

Case 11/70 *Internationale Handelsgesellschaft* [1970] ECR 1125 (Fundamental rights; general principles of law).

Cases 166/73, 146/73 *Rheinmühlen I, II* [1974] ECR 33 and 139 (Extent to which national courts are bound by rulings of superior courts).

Case 4/73 *Nold* [1974] ECR 491 (Fundamental rights; general principles of law; common constitutional traditions).

Case 36/75 *Rutili* [1975] ECR 1219 (Equal treatment; reference to the ECHR).

Case 175/73 *Amalgamated European Public Service Union* [1974] ECR 917 (Freedom to form associations).

Case 130/75 *Prais* [1976] ECR 1589 (Freedom of religion).

Joined Cases 117/76 and 16/77 *Quellmehl* [1977] ECR 1753 (Principle of equality).

Case 149/77 *Defrenne* [1978] ECR 1365 (Fundamental rights; general principles of law).

Case 44/79 *Hauer* [1979] ECR 3727 (Fundamental rights; right to property).

Case 85/79 *Hoffmann-La Roche* [1979] ECR 461 (Fundamental rights; principle of the right to be heard).

Joined Cases 154, 205, 206, 227-228, 263 and 264/78, 39, 31, 83 and 85/79 *Valsabbia* [1980] ECR 907 (Fundamental rights; right of property).

Case 293/83 *Gravier* [1985] ECR 593 (Equal treatment; students' registration fee).

Case 234/85 *Keller* [1986] ECR 2897 (Freedom to pursue one's trade or profession).

Case 12/86 *Demirel* [1987] ECR 3719 (Fundamental rights; Convention on Human Rights).

Joined Cases 46/87 and 227/88 *Hoechst* [1989] ECR 2919 (Fundamental rights; natural justice; administrative procedure; inviolability of the home).

Case 374/87 *Orkem* [1989] ECR 3343 (Fundamental rights; natural justice; investigation procedure).

Case 265/87 *Schräder* [1989] ECR 2263 (Rights of ownership; freedom to engage in business; restrictions).

Case 100/88 *Oyowe and Traore* [1989] ECR 4304 (Fundamental rights; freedom of expression).

Case 5/88 *Wachauf* [1989] ECR 2633 (Restrictions on fundamental rights).

Case C-62/90 *Commission v Germany,* judgment given on 8.4.1992, not yet reported (Fundamental rights; observance by Member States; restrictions on grounds of the public interest).

Case C-219/91 *Ter Voort,* judgment given on 28.10.1992, not yet reported (Freedom of expression).

Case C-97/91 *Borelli,* judgment given on 3.12.1992, not yet reported (Fundamental rights; right to take action in the courts).

Case C-357/89 *Raulin,* judgment given on 26.2.1992, not yet reported (Equal treatment; prohibition on nationality discrimination).

■ GENERAL PRINCIPLES OF LAW (SELECTION)

Legal certainty

Joined Cases 18 and 35/65 *Gutmann* [1966] ECR 103, 149 et seq.
Case 78/74 *Deuka* [1975] ECR 421.
Case 98/78 *Racke* [1979] ECR 69.
Case 96/78 *Decker* [1979] ECR 101.
Case 265/78 *Ferwerda* [1980] ECR 617.
Case 61/79 *Denkavit* [1980] ECR 1205.

Joined Cases 66, 127 and 128/79 *Salumi* [1980] ECR 1237.
Case 826/79 *Mireco* [1980] ECR 2559.
Case 70/83 *Kloppenburg* [1984] ECR 1075.
Case 257/86 *Commission v Italy* [1988] ECR 3249.
Joined Cases 92 and 93/87 *Commission v France and United Kingdom* [1989] ECR 437.

Proportionality

Case 114/76 *Bela-Mühle* [1977] ECR 1211.
Case 116/76 *Granaria* [1977] ECR 1247.
Case 8/77 *Sagulo* [1977] ECR 1495.
Case 122/78 *Buitoni* [1979] ECR 677.
Case 154/78 *Valsabbia* [1980] ECR 907.
Case 808/79 *Pardini* [1980] ECR 2103.
Case 125/83 *Corman* [1985] ECR 3039.
Case 181/84 *Man (Sugar)* [1985] ECR 2889.
Case 21/85 *Maas* [1986] ECR 3537.
Case 265/87 *Schräder* [1989] ECR 2263.
Case C-8/89 *Zardi* [1990] ECR I-2529.
Case C-331/89 *Fedesa* [1990] ECR I-4057.

Protection of legitimate expectations

Case 74/74 *CNTA* [1975] ECR 533.
Case 97/76 *Merkur* [1977] ECR 1063.
Case 78/77 *Lührs* [1978] ECR 169.
Case 90/77 *Stimming* [1978] ECR 995.
Joined Cases 12, 18 and 21/77 *Debayser* [1978] ECR 553.
Joined Cases 205-215/82 *Deutsche Milchkontor* [1983] ECR 2633.
Case 120/86 *Mulder* [1988] ECR 2321.
Case 170/86 *von Deetzen* [1988] ECR 2355.
Case 316/88 *Krücken* [1988] ECR 2233.
Case C-350/88 *Delacre* [1990] ECR I-418.

FURTHER READING

■ COMMUNITY PUBLICATIONS

☐ *Community law*
Offprint from the General Report on the Activities of the Communities. ECSC, EEC, EAEC, Commission. Luxembourg: EC annual since 1967

Louis, J.-V.:
☐ *The Community Legal Order (second edition)*
European perspectives
Luxembourg, EC, Commission, 1983

☐ *Thirty years of Community law*
European perspectives. Luxembourg, EC, Commission, XXV, 498 pp., 1982

■ OTHER PUBLICATIONS

Alves, J. J.:
☐ *Lições de direito comunitário.*
2 vol., Coimbra, Coimbra Editora, 1989, 1992, 470 + 334 pp.

Audretsch, H. A. H.:
☐ *Supervision in European Community law. Observance by the Member States of their treaty obligations*
A treatise on international and supranational supervision (second edition) Amsterdam, North Holland, 1986, xx, 782 pp.

Barav, A. (Edited by):
☐ *Commentary on the EEC Treaty and the Single European Act.*
Oxford, Clarendon Press, 1993, 900 pp.

Berr, Boulouis et autres:
☐ *Études de droit des Communautés européennes*
Mélanges offerts à Pierre-Henri Teitgen, Paris Pedone, 1984, XXIV, 527 p.

Beutler, Bengt; Bieber, Roland; Pipkorn, Jörn; Streil, Jochen:
☐ *Die Europäische Gemeinschaft — Rechtsordnung und Politik*
3. Auflage, Baden-Baden: Nomos, 1987. 587 S.

Bieber, Roland; Ress, Georg (Hrsg.):
☐ *Die Dynamik des Europäischen Gemeinschaftsrechts*
Baden-Baden, Nomos, 1987, 587 S.

Bieber-Schwarze:
☐ *Verfassungsentwicklung in der Europäischen Gemeinschaft*
Baden-Baden, 1984

Bleckmann, Albert:
☐ *Europarecht — Das Recht der Europäischen Wirtschaftsgemeinschaft*
5. Auflage, Köln, Heymann, 1990, 917 S.

Brinkhorst, L.J. — Barents, R.:
☐ *Grondlijnen van Europees recht.*
5de druk, Alphen aan de Rijn (etc.) Samsom H.D. Tjeenk Willink, 1990, 222 blz.

Boulouis, J.:
☐ *Grands arrêts de la Cour de Justice des Communautés européennes.*
Tome 1: Caractères généraux du droit communautaire, droit institutionnel, contrôle juridictionnel. 5e éd., 1991, 470 p.
Tome 2: Libre circulation des marchandises des personnes, des services et des capitaux Concurrence. Dispositions fiscales. Agriculture, Transports, Politiques économique, commerciale, sociale.
3e éd. Dalioz, Paris, 1991, 511 p.

Boulouis, Jean:
- *Droit institutionnel des Communautés européennes.*
4e édition, Montchrestien, Paris, 1993

Bredimas, Anna:
- *Methods of interpretation and Community law.*
European Studies in law, Amsterdam, North Holland, 1978, xviii, 219 pp.

Cappelletti, Mauro; Seccombe, Monica; Weiler, Joseph (Edited by):
- *Integration through Law. Europe and the American Federal Experience.*
3 vols, Berlin/New York, De Gruyter, 1986

Cartou, Louis:
- *Communautés européennes*
9e édition, Dalloz, Paris, 1989, xxii, 808 p.

Constantinesco, Leontin-Jean:
- *Das Recht der Europäischen Gemeinschaften.*
Band 1: Das institutionelle Recht, Baden-Baden, Nomos, 1977, 922 S.

Constantinesco, V. e.a.:
- *Traité instituant la CEE. Commentaire par articles.*
Economica, Paris, 1992, 1648 p.

Deuses, Manfred (Hrsg.):
- *Handbuch des EG-Wirtschaftsrechts.*
München, C. H. Beck, Loseblattsammlung, 1993

Deniau, Jean-François:
- *Le marché commun.*
14e édition, PUF, Paris, 1989, 128 p.

Due, Ole; Lando, Ole; von Eyben, W. E. (eds):
- *Karnovs EF-samling.*
2. udg., København, Karnov, 1978, xi, 1090 s.

Grabitz, Eberhard:
- *EWG-Kommentar.*
München, C. H. Beck, Loseblattsammlung, 1986

Grabitz, E. (Hrsg.):
- *Abgestufte Integration — eine Alternative zum herkömmlichen Integrationskonzept?*
Kehl/Straßburg, N.P. Engel, IX, 411 S.

Von der Groeben, Hans; von Boeckh, Hans; Thiesing, Jochen; Ehlermann, Claus Dieter:
- *Kommentar zum EWG-Vertrag.*
4. Auflage, 4 Bände, Baden-Baden, 1991, Nomos, 6449 S.

Hallstein, W.:
- *Die Europäische Gemeinschaft*
5. Auflage, Düsseldorf/Wien, 1979

Hartley, T. C.:
- *The foundations of European Community law. An introduction to the constitutional and administrative law of the European Community*
Second edition, Oxford, Clarendon, 1988, xxxiv, 551 pp.

Hilf, Meinhard:
- *Die Organisationsstruktur der Europäischen Gemeinschaften*
Berlin-New York, Springer, XVII, 442 S.

Ipsen, Hans-Peter:
- *Europäisches Gemeinschaftsrecht.*
Tübingen, Mohr, 1972, 1092 S.

Isaac, Guy:
- *Droit communautaire général*
3e édition, Masson, Paris, 1990, 318 p.

Jacqué, J. P.; Bieber, R.; Constantinesco, V.; Nickel, D.:
- *Le Parlement européen.*
Economica, Paris, 1984, 286 p.

Kapteyn, P.J.G. & VerLoren van Themaat, P.:
- *Introduction to the law of the European Communities after the coming into force of the Single European Act*
Edited by L. W. Gormley (second edition), Deventer, Kluwer/Graham & Trotman, 1989, xxvi, 927 pp.

Lasok, D. & Bridge, J. W.:
- *The law and institutions of the European Communities.*
(Fifth edition), London, Butterworths, 1991, LXXXIX, 591 pp.

Lauria F.:
- *Manuale di diritto delle Comunità europee.*
Torino, UTET, 1990, VIII, 344 p.

Maresceau, Marc:
- ☐ *De directe werking van het Europese gemeenschapsrecht.*
Europese monografieën, Deventer, Kluwer, 1978, 330 blz.

Mathijsen, P.S.R.F.:
- ☐ *A guide to European Economic Community law.*
Preface by J. D. B. Mitchell. (Fifth edition) London, Sweet & Maxwell, 1990, LVII, 343 pp.

Mégret, Jacques; Louis, Jean-Victor; Vignes, Daniel; Waelbroeck, Michel:
- ☐ *Commentaire Mégret. Le droit de la Communauté économique européenne.*
Bruxelles, Éditions de l'Université Libre de Bruxelles, 1970-1986, 15 volumes, 2e édition 1990 en cours d'édition.

Molina Del Pozo, C.F.:
- ☐ *Manual de derecho de la Comunidad Europea.*
2a ed., Madrid, Editorial Trivium, 1990, 609 p.

Nicolaysen, Gert:
- ☐ *Europarecht I.*
Baden-Baden, 1991, Nomos, 267 S. (völlige Neubearbeitung des Ersten Teils des Studienbuchs von 1979).

Oppermann, Thomas:
- ☐ *Europarecht*
München, C. H. Beck, 1991

Parry, Anthony; Hardy, Stephen:
- ☐ *EEC law.*
(Second edition) (With James Dinnage) London, Sweet & Maxwell, 1981, lvi, 531 pp.

Pennacchini, E.; Monaco, R.; Ferrari Bravo, L. (ed.):
- ☐ *Manuale di diritto comunitario.*
(2^a ed.), Torino, 1983, 1272 pag.

Plender, Richard:
- ☐ *A practical introduction to European Community law.*
London, Sweet & Maxwell, 1980, xxiii, 166 pp.

Pocar, Fausto:
- ☐ *Diritto delle Comunità europee.*
(4^a ed.) Milano, Giuffrè, 1991, xxx, 372 pag.

Quadri, Rolando; Monaco, Riccardo; Trabucchi, Alberto:
- ☐ *Trattato istitutivo della Comunità economica europea. Commentario.*
4 vol., Milano, Giuffrè, 1965

Quadri, Rolando; Monaco, Riccardo; Trabucchi, Alberto:
- ☐ *Trattato istitutivo della Comunità europea del carbone e dell'acciaio. Commentario.*
3 vol., Milano, Giuffrè, 1970.

Röttinger, M., Weyringer, C., u. a.:
- ☐ *Handbuch der europäischen Integration.*
Wien, Manz'sche Verlags- und Universitätsbuchhandlung, 1991, 1079 S.

Schermers:
- ☐ *Judicial Protection in the European Communities*
(5th ed.), Deventer, Kluwer, 1991, xviii, 585 p.

Schweizer, Michael, und Hummer, Waldemar:
- ☐ *Europarecht.*
3. Auflage, 1990, Neuwied (etc.), Metzner Verlag, 476 S.

Thiel, Elke:
- ☐ *Die Europäische Gemeinschaft zwischen Krise und Bewährung.*
2. Auflage, 1985, Hamburg

Weidenfeld, W.; Wessels, W. (Hrsg.):
- ☐ *Jahrbuch der europäischen Integration.*
Bonn (erscheint jährlich).

Wyatt, Derrick; Dashwood, Allan:
- ☐ *The substantive law of the EEC.*
(Second edition) London, Sweet & Maxwell, 1987, 549 pp.

European Commission
Rue de la Loi 200, B-1049 Bruxelles

BELGIQUE/BELGIË
Rue Archimède 73
B-1040 BRUXELLES
Archimedesstraat 73
B-1040 BRUSSEL
Tél. (32-2) 295 38 44
Télex 26 657 COMINF B
Fax (32-2) 295 01 66

DANMARK
Højbrohus
Østergade 61
Postbox 144
DK-1004 KØBENHAVN K
Tlf. (45) 33 14 41 40
Telex 16 402 COMEUR DK
Fax (45) 33 11 12 03/14 13 92 (sekretariat)
     (45) 33 14 14 47 (dokumentation)

BUNDESREPUBLIK DEUTSCHLAND
Zitelmannstraße 22
D-53113 BONN
Postfach 53106 BONN
Tel. (49-228) 53 00 90
Fernschreiber (041) 88 66 48 EUROP D
Fernkopie (49-228) 53 00 950/12

Kurfürstendamm 102
D-10711 BERLIN
Tel. (49-30) 896 09 30
Fernschreiber (041) 18 40 15 EUROP D
Fernkopie (49-30) 892 20 59

Erhardtstraße 27
D-80331 MÜNCHEN
Tel. (49-89) 202 10 11
Fernschreiber (041) 52 18 135
Fernkopie (49-89) 202 10 15

GREECE/ΕΛΛΑΔΑ
Vassilissis Sofias 2
T.K. 30 284
GR-106 74 ATHINA
Tel. (30-1) 725 10 00
Telex (0601) 219 324 ECAT GR
Telefax (30-1) 724 46 20

ESPAÑA
Calle de Serrano, 41, 5ª
E-28001 MADRID
Tel. (34-1) 435 17 00
Télex (052) 46 818 OIPE E
Fax (34-1) 576 03 87

Av. Diagonal, 407 bis, 18ª
E-08008 BARCELONA
Tel. (34-3) 415 81 77 (5 líneas)
Télex (052) 97 524 BDC E
Fax (34-3) 415 63 11

FRANCE
288, boulevard Saint-Germain
F-75007 PARIS
Tél. (33-1) 40 63 38 00
Télex 202 271 F CCE BRF
Fax (33-1) 45 56 94 17/18/19

CMCI
2, rue Henri Barbusse
F-13241 MARSEILLE Cedex 01
Tél. (33) 91 91 46 00
Télex (042) 402 538 EURMA
Fax (33) 91 90 98 07

IRELAND
Jean Monnet Centre
39 Molesworth Street
DUBLIN 2
Tel. (353-1) 671 22 44
Fax (353-1) 671 26 57

ITALIA
Via Poli, 29
I-00187 ROMA
Tel. (39-6) 699 991
Telex (043) 610 184 EUROMA I
Telecopia (39-6) 679 16 58/679 36 52

Corso Magenta, 59
I-20123 MILANO
Tel. (39-2) 48 01 25 05
Telex (043) 316 200 EURMIL I
Telecopia (39-2) 481 85 43

LUXEMBOURG
Bâtiment Jean Monnet
rue Alcide De Gasperi
L-2920 LUXEMBOURG
Tél. (352) 43 01-1
Télex 3423/3446/3476 COMEUR LU
Fax (352) 43 01-344 33

NEDERLAND
Korte Vijverberg 5
NL-2513 AB DEN HAAG
Postbus 30465
NL-2500 GL DEN HAAG
Tel. (31-70) 346 93 26
Telex 31 094 EURCO NL
Telefax (31-70) 364 66 19

PORTUGAL
Centro Europeu Jean Monnet
Largo Jean Monnet, 1-10.º
P-1200 LISBOA
Tel. (351-1) 350 98 00
 — lignes directes: 350 98...
Telex (0404) 18 810 COMEUR P
Telecópia (351-1) 355 43 97/
   /350 98 01/350 98 02/350 98 03

UNITED KINGDOM
Jean Monnet House
8 Storey's Gate
LONDON SW1P 3AT
Tel. (44-71) 973 19 92
Telex (051) 23208 EURUK G
Fax (44-71) 973 19 00/19 10/18 95

Windsor House
9/15 Bedford Street
BELFAST BT2 7EG
Tel. (44-232) 24 07 08
Telex (051) 74117 CECBEL G
Fax (44-232) 24 82 41

4 Cathedral Road
CARDIFF CF1 9SG
Tel. (44-222) 37 16 31
Telex (051) 497727 EUROPA G
Fax (44-222) 39 54 89

9 Alva Street
EDINBURGH EH2 4PH
Tel. (44-31) 225 20 58
Telex (051) 727420 EUEDIN G
Fax (44-31) 226 41 05

ÖSTERREICH
Hoyosgasse 5
A-1040 WIEN
Tel. (43-1) 505 33 79/505 34 91
Telex (047) 133152 EUROP A
Fax (43-1) 505 33 797

SUOMI/FINLAND
Pohoisesplanadi 31
PO Box 234
SF-00100 HELSINKI
Tel. (358-0) 65 64 20
Fax (358-0) 65 67 28

NORGE
Postboks 1643 Vika 0119 Oslo 1
Haakon's VII Gate No 6
N-0161 OSLO 1
Tel. (47-22) 83 35 83
Telex (056) 79967 COMEU N
Fax (47-22) 83 40 55

SVERIGE
PO Box 16396
Hamngatan 6
S-11147 STOCKHOLM
Tel. (46-8) 611 11 72
Telex (054) 134 49
Fax (46-8) 20 44 35

UNITED STATES OF AMERICA
2100 M Street, NW
7th floor
WASHINGTON, DC 20037
Tel. (202) 862 95 00
Telex (023) 64215 EURCOM UW
Fax (202) 429 17 66

3 Dag Hammarskjöld Plaza
305 East 47th Street
NEW YORK, NY 10017
Tel. (212) 371 38 04
Telex 012396 EURCOM NY
Fax (212) 758 27 18/688 10 13

NIPPON
Europa House
9-15 Sanbancho
Chiyoda-Ku
TOKYO 102
Tel. (813) 239 04 41
Telex (072) 28567 COMEUTOK J
Fax (813) 32 39 93 37/32 61 51 94

European Commission

THE ABC OF COMMUNITY LAW

Fourth edition

Luxembourg: Office for Official Publications of the European Communities

1994 — 69 pp. — 16.2 x 22.9 cm

European Documentation series — 1993

ISBN 92-826-6293-4

Booklet intended mainly for non-lawyers. Tries to explain the European legal order in layman's language.